"Glorify Your name,
not ours, O Lord!
Cause everyone
to praise your lovingkindness
and your truth."
Psalm 115:1

How Green is My Mountain

Ruth Klaasen

InterVarsity Press
Downers Grove
Illinois 60515

InterVarsity Press is the book-
publishing division of Inter-Varsity
Christian Fellowship, a student
movement active on campus at
hundreds of universities, colleges
and schools of nursing.
For information about local and
regional activities, write
IVCF, 233 Langdon St.,
Madison, WI 53703.

Distributed in Canada through
InterVarsity Press, 1875 Leslie St.,
Unit 10, Don Mills,
Ontario M3B 2M5, Canada.

All Scripture quotations are from
The Living Bible.© 1971 by Tyndale
House Publishers, Wheaton,
Illinois. Used by permission.

ISBN 0-87784-561-1

Library of Congress
Catalog Card Number:79-1646

Printed in the United States of America

For The Sunday Night Group
The Philippines
and
The Monday Night Group
Berkeley, California, 1976-1977,
who cared, loved and prayed for us.

Very Special Thanks
to
Walt and Ginny Hearn,
Berkeley, California,
editors,
and
Moira Bell,
Newport-on-Tay, Scotland,
secretary,
as well as all
the other members of
The Monday Night Group
and most especially, my husband,
without whose
practical help and spiritual gifts
this story would not have been told
until eternity!

Prologue

How did we get abroad in the first place? Simple. We wanted to go. Ever since we were little kids reading books about life in other countries, we wanted to travel. Growing up in tightly knit Mennonite communities in Saskatchewan, Canada, our only main opportunity to hear about and see the outside world was through missionaries' visits with their slides and curios.

Our first significant opportunity to get to know international students was as undergraduates at the University of Saskatchewan. We participated in the International Students' Club, the Banff International Christmas and the Canada-India Association. Having foreign students as roommates—or best of all, as friends—convinced us that we wanted to see how the rest of the world lived.

During Mark's graduate work at Trent and McGill Universities, students from other countries joined us in small Bible study groups. Some of them were much more mature believers than we were. They gently taught us about discipleship in a cross-cultural setting.

Mark pursued graduate work because he wanted to teach at the university level. He had been deeply impressed by the impact of Christian professors on his life. He wanted to give that same quality of encouragement to others struggling with the age-old questions of life's meaning and purpose in an environment so often hostile to God.

Because of our associations with Inter-Varsity Christian Fellowship, we went several times to the triennial student missionary conventions held in Urbana, Illinois. Those conferences opened our eyes to various opportunities that believers with professional skills could have in a country other than their own.

When Mark was nearing the end of his Ph.D. research in insect ecology, he started to apply for teaching positions in various countries. Nothing seemed to work out. They all wanted someone with at least five years of teaching experience.

At that time the director of an international research institute in the Philippines was traveling through Canada looking for several newly hatched Ph.D.'s who could be trained in various aspects of research on rice. He interviewed Mark but they agreed that they were mutually not interested. Mark wanted a teaching post. The director wanted a research scientist in a slightly different aspect of entomology.

As graduation loomed closer, however, with no job offers, Mark decided to write that institute and ask if they had found an entomologist for their empty post. If not, he might be willing to shift somewhat his area of interest in order to do entomological research for them. He got an immediate reply by telegram: "Can you come to the Philippines for an interview in two weeks? Cable reply immediately."

That night over Cantonese food in a French-Canadian village restaurant, we agonized over the unanticipated offer.

We had always thought that teaching was Mark's gift. He had endured the research aspect of his graduate work in order to get that Ph.D., his "union card" into the university. Now came the possibility of doing research abroad instead of the longed-for teaching post. We felt that we must be seriously considering the job if he took the interview trip. He couldn't go just as a lark. If he took the trip and was offered the job, would he have to accept it? All other doors seemed closed. Now an unexpected one had swung open. Why?

Like Gideon, we decided to put out a fleece. Mark would go for the interview and would look over the situation. If he was offered the job and if the salary was enough for us to live on and if no other teaching jobs became available in the next month, we would accept that position as God's will for our lives.

The Montreal-Manila round trip was made in eight days. Mark returned weary, confused and with many reservations. It appeared to be a high-pressure position. The scientists seemed to be provided with everything needed to do top-quality work. First-class equipment, plenty of well-trained support staff and a year-round growing season. Although the staff was international, their housing was palatial and American-style compared with the Filipinos who lived in the nearby college town. They were also "marked" by the white air-conditioned Fords with special license plates in which they were chauffeured around. While there, Mark had suffered an acute attack of hay fever.

All those considerations left us decidedly uncomfortable. Could a job in that kind of place be God's will for a pair of Mennonite believers so well schooled in the merits of simple lifestyle? Besides, we had listened to so many international students protest the luxurious lifestyle of expatriate scientists and missionaries in their countries.

But there was still that "wet fleece on the dry ground" to be remembered. The salary was certainly more than our Asian friends had told us would be adequate. When the job offer came in the mail three weeks later, we sat on it for another week until the month time limit was up. We were desperately praying that if it wasn't the place for us, another offer would come immediately. None came.

A visitor, however, did come. Ku, a Malaysian believer, preparing to teach Indian and Eskimo children in the Canadian Northwest, was our house guest that week. He counseled us, saying, "Perhaps like Joseph, this is your Egypt. Go down, and like Joseph, obey God carefully in all you do."

We mailed Mark's acceptance letter. One week later, an offer for a teaching post in the Middle East arrived. Our emotional struggle was intense but brief. We knew by now that the Philippines was the place for us. "This is the way, walk in it," says the Lord, your God.

Almost a year later we stepped out onto the burning concrete, engulfed in the ovenlike tropical sun, at Manila International Airport. The adventure had begun.

This is the story of how a loving heavenly Father worked in the life of one person, one couple, one family—in a culture foreign to their own—so that he could work through them.

1

Unto Us Two Sons Were Given

My head lay cradled in a pillow on my husband's lap. Today I didn't even notice the Ford's poor shock absorbers as our driver carefully inched his way over the patchy concrete road toward Manila.

Outside, a typhoon was raging. I watched the sheets of rain lash the car windows, but was content. Mark gently patted my head and asked with typical husbandly anxiety, "Are you all right, Wifey?" I loved Mark to call me Wifey.

I smiled, and replied, "Oh, yes." I closed my eyes and snuggled into the pillow. The word from my Lord was sure: I would get there on time—his appointed time for me.

Another searing contraction wound around me. I checked my watch. Seven minutes since the last one. Manila was still at least an hour away if we could drive steadily. "You will be at the right place at the right time." I took a deep breath and marveled at the calmness I felt. It was all so unreal. It just wasn't my kind of calmness.

This had been no ordinary pregnancy. No pregnancy ever is, when it's your own and the first one at that.

From the start we seemed to have more struggles in deciding whether to have children than most of the young couples we knew. All the factors had been turned over and over. Would becoming parents be the best use of our time? In this age of overpopulation was it right to have children when we could adopt them? Did we have a right to have children of our own just to see what we could create?

Then at a Faith at Work Conference we heard Lionel Whiston, author of *Are You Fun to Live With?*, tell how God had broken, led and taught him through the gift of his children. That was a totally new concept to us. From our limited listening and observations, it seemed that many parents thought of their children as burdens, hard work, expense and responsibilities—not gifts.

Just at that point in our lives a doctoral thesis had to be completed and typed, and a new job was waiting. It was hardly a convenient time to have all one's neatly formed concepts about parenting shattered, to have to admit to God and each other that maybe our thinking on the matter had to be changed.

The thesis was duly completed by my husband and typed by me. The day came when he took six neatly compiled copies down to the Graduate Faculty Office and I took a different bus to see my doctor.

It just couldn't be true. Why, I had felt no discomfort, no nausea, no unusual fatigue. I'd been working late hours typing and packing when, according to the books, I should have been uncomfortable if not miserable. Our Lord's timing was perfect. He convinced us that this baby was his gift. That awareness never left us through the next months of waiting.

Upon arrival in the Philippines we quickly found a reputable doctor. In the fifth month of my pregnancy my uterus started to contract for no apparent reason. The doctor was alarmed. The contractions signified to her that the fetus was attempting to abort.

An emotional struggle ensued for us. This baby was God's gift. We were sure of that. If God chose to take it from us now, we dared not try to fight against him. But how very much we wanted the baby.

Finally, we bowed our wills and prayed: "Lord Jesus, you know how much we long for this baby. You are the one who allowed it to be conceived at the time you chose. You have given us love and longing for it. Thank you that you know what is best. Your will be done. Amen."

At about the same time, I was beginning to feel uncomfortable about a lack of rapport with my doctor. I told myself that I was spoiled because all my previous doctors had been personal friends. This woman had an excellent medical reputation, but with her huge practice, she couldn't give me the individual attention I was used to having.

I went for my seven-month checkup as scheduled while Mark was on a fact-finding trip to what was then East Pakistan. Everything about the visit seemed negative between the doctor and me. When I stepped on the scale, she was upset. "You have gained ten pounds since your last visit. It is too much. You must have forgotten the diet I asked you to follow, no? You must lose five pounds before your next visit." Her mouth was set in a straight line and her face looked pained.

I felt very uncomfortable. "But Doctor, I followed it, but—" It was no use, her back was turned toward me, and she hurried from the examining room. Her nurse smiled sympathetically and helped me into my clothes.

Minutes later, seated across from the doctor in her office, I ventured to ask about her preferences in methods of childbirth and drugs used for anesthesia. I wanted assurance from her that the birth process would be as natural as possible.

She looked at me strangely, "Why do you ask?" and continued sternly, "I am your doctor. I will take care of you. But since you asked, I prefer to use twilight sleep from the first labor pain and total anesthesia for the birth." Her tone sof-

tened, "You are over thirty years old—much too old to be
having your first baby. We will make it as easy as possible,
yes?"

"But Doctor," I protested, "remember I told you my husband has many allergies that affect the respiratory tract. I've
read that twilight sleep can depress the respiratory systems of
new borns, and if our child has inherited those allergies. . . ."
My voice trailed off. I knew I wasn't communicating.

"Nurse," commanded the doctor firmly, "please book Mrs.
Klaasen for an appointment in two weeks and call my next
patient."

I left depressed and convinced that it was unwise for me to
continue under her care.

Mark returned from East Pakistan a few days before fight-
ing broke out there. How very grateful I was to have him back!
We agreed that I should switch to an obstetrician with whom
I would feel more relaxed.

I had heard of a mission hospital that had several obstetri-
cians on staff. One doctor in particular encouraged childbirth
to be as natural as possible. I immediately called and booked
an appointment for the first possible opportunity, a Sunday
afternoon one week later.

All through that week of waiting for the appointment I had
a serene sense of God's peace. This would be the right doctor.
I would see him at the right time. It was also a week of
typhoon weather. That made waiting more difficult, but
through it all, what unnatural peace I knew.

Finally Sunday came. Just before leaving, the "bag of water"
broke. "This simply cannot be," I thought. "It just can't be
true. I can't be in labor!"

The driver arrived and we left for Manila. It took almost
two hours to make the forty-five-mile trip. The contractions
were constant, though irregular.

"Am I really in labor?" I asked myself as I paced the floor
outside of Dr. Morell's office.

Finally, the Filipino nurse opened the door and called, "Dr.
Morell is ready to see you, Mrs. Klaasen." I gulped. I had

waited for this moment for over a week.

I was so afraid of having a baby, alone, in a strange country without my mother near me. Would I be able to put my trust in this missionary doctor? Would he allow my husband to stay with me throughout the labor? Would he give me, against my will, the drugs that I feared would endanger the birth of our baby? Would he take my fears seriously?

It took but a few minutes to have all those fears alleviated. Dr. Morell was gracious about everything—about our being there to see him on an exploratory visit; about the disagreement I had had with my other doctor over the twilight sleep medication. It *was* a danger, he concurred, since the baby might have inherited Mark's respiratory allergies.

Dr. Morell assured us he believed that labor and birth should be as natural as possible. We heaved a great sigh of relief.

Outside, the typhoon gathered in intensity. Dr. Morell checked me over and announced: "You are in labor now. You two will be parents before midnight."

How could that be? Our baby, two months premature?

I checked into the Manila Sanitarium and Hospital. My husband filled out the reams of entrance forms and comforted and encouraged me. The nurse in attendance couldn't believe the swiftness of the labor, so Dr. Morell was summoned.

Transfer to the delivery room was swift. Dr. Morell came flying up the back steps, leaving his supper. There was hardly time to scrub. He deftly administered the spinal block.

Moments later he said, "It's not a full-term head."

Suddenly I knew. I knew why I had always been so famished. Why there had been all that circuslike activity inside.

"I know," I replied calmly, "there are two. Have you got the incubators ready?"

"Yes," he assured me, "we have several in the hospital."

Moments later the delivery room staff chorused together: "It's a boy!"

He howled all that his three pounds eight ounces could yell. Stephen Mark Klaasen had arrived. I was euphoric. At long last, Opa Klaasen had his *Thronfolger,* Grandfather's "heir to the throne," and we had the gift of a son.

It wasn't over. The other baby took ten long minutes to emerge. Another son. What a fantastic gift. Twin sons! The second one had difficulty breathing and it seemed to take an agonizingly long time until I heard his wail. When it pierced the air, I relaxed and prayed, "Thank you! Thank you, Jesus!"

Not long afterward I was reunited with my husband. Dr. Morell joined us. We appreciated his warm congratulations. He was gently candid, however, about the survival of the twins, each weighing under four pounds.

"The first forty-eight hours are crucial," he said. "They were born under the best conditions for survival. If any more anesthesia had been given, their underdeveloped respiratory systems wouldn't have had a chance. We'll just have to wait and pray."

And how we did pray! We were so confident, however, that they would live. They were God's gifts to us. Surely, after these months of finding him so real in the waiting period, now he wouldn't take them from us.

We had to choose another name. As we leafed through the Gospels in search of a name with a meaningful biblical legacy, Andrew appealed to us. In each Gospel, we noted that when the Lord Jesus called Andrew, it said that he came quickly. That was exactly what we wanted for our son, a quick response to Jesus when he called.

The first twenty-four hours passed. The pediatrician brought reports: both were holding their own.

Monday evening, I triumphantly, but painfully, made the walk to the nursery. I just had to see my sons again. I shuddered when I saw all the necessary tubing sticking into their tiny bodies.

Later my husband arrived, puffed with pride from a day of receiving congratulations. Now we rejoiced together. Our little boys were holding their own and their first twenty-four hours were over. We spent a peaceful evening together gratefully praising God for the gift of twenty-four hours of life for our sons and the love of our friends.

Early the next morning I checked on the babies. All was well, and so I decided to send a radio message to my husband in the province that he need not make the long trip back into Manila that evening to visit us.

Later in the day, the special nurses informed me that it seemed that Andrew had stopped breathing for a fraction of a second several times during the night. But they didn't think it was serious.

That afternoon many visitors kept me away from my vigil at the nursery window. Finally, I was able to go down to see the babies.

What I saw frightened me. The pediatrician and several residents were there. They had partially drawn the curtains around Andrew and were very intent in their discussions about our son. They didn't see me, but I knew from the looks on their faces that all was not well. Back in my room, I wept.

Suddenly I remembered that my husband wasn't coming that evening to be with me. Panic struck. Quickly I tried to reach the institute's Manila office by telephone. The secretary was gentle. She would try to radio or telephone long-distance.

Minutes later she called back, having been unable to reach my husband. Mark won't come, I thought. Maybe his son will die tonight and he won't be here to see him one more time or to be with me. I was alone. Desperately alone. Would God hear my prayer and answer my need? Sobbing, I asked Jesus to come to my need and help me.

Minutes later the bedside telephone rang. It was Mark. His cheery voice cut my ragged emotions. Through my tears I told him to please come immediately. Andrew was slipping away. Poor Mark. He was in a suburb of Manila twenty minutes from the hospital getting a haircut and had just sent his driver to eat supper.

Our Lord had guided Mark to disregard my earlier radio message. He had toyed with my suggestion, but decided he wanted to come anyway just to be with us. Now he would be here in the hour of deepest need in our five years of marriage.

The driver was located and Mark was soon beside me.

He was hardly in when the pediatrician arrived. We knew what she would say. We tried to remain as calm and matter-of-fact as she. Our second son was suffering from severe apnea. He had stopped breathing many times all afternoon. His little heart was very strong and it kept on beating. She thought, however, he would die in a quarter of an hour. She left.

We buried our faces in my pillow and wept. Death tore chunks out of our hearts that evening. Grief is bitter.

Much later, we bent our wills and prayed, "Father God, we don't want to accept your will for us, but we choose to now." A ray of peace pierced our sorrow then. We began to think about arrangements for Andrew's funeral.

We asked the Holy Spirit to guide us so that through Andrew's death others would be brought to think about God. We had named our son Andrew because we longed that he would come quickly when Jesus called him. Jesus had called him quickly, and quickly our son had gone.

Word was sent back to our provincial home through our driver that we would arrive with the tiny coffin the next day at noon. We asked our new Filipino Christian friends to make the necessary arrangements for us.

The staff at the Manila San was so helpful. The supervisor of the laundry, a carpenter, built and painted a white casket during the night and prepared the wasted body for burial. John Lockhart, a missionary friend, offered to come and speak the message of Romans 8:28 to all of us.

Our trip back to the province with the Lockharts was filled with subdued, but thank-filled conversation. We remembered that we had been at the right hospital with the right doctor at the right time on Sunday evening.

Physically the birth of our twins had been easy for me. Additional anesthesia had been unnecessary for me, so now Stephen would have the best possible chance for survival. We remembered the Christian care and concern of the staff. We knew they had done everything humanly possible to save Andrew. They could be trusted to do the same for the surviving son in the incubator. We were grateful that Mark had disregarded my radio message and had come to Manila the evening before. The Lord had not left me alone.

On arrival in our town, we found that our Christian friends had all been contacted for the memorial service for Andrew. Some of Mark's Sunday school students had gathered fragrant waxy-white plumeria blossoms and shaped them into a three-foot cross to lay over the coffin.

In a beautiful way, "Papa John" Lockhart impressed upon us that Andrew's death was part of God's magnificent plan. Because God had a higher purpose for Andrew than to let him live and grow up, he had taken him soon after his birth. God could be more perfectly glorified through Andrew's death. God loved us. All things would work together for good for God and us.

We were sure of the fact that God loved us. That had been the only fact anchoring us in the turbulent sea of our emotions. We wanted to affirm it to our friends assembled that noon hour. My husband and I rose to sing:

Jesus, I am resting, resting
In the joy of what Thou art;
I am finding out the greatness
Of Thy loving heart.

Singing John Pigott's hymn was one of the most difficult things I've ever done, but as we reached the third stanza, our voices became more steady:

Simply trusting Thee, Lord Jesus,
I behold Thee as Thou art,
And Thy love, so pure, so changeless,
Satisfies my heart;
Satisfies its deepest longings,
Meets, supplies its every need,
Compasseth me round with blessings:
Thine is love indeed!

Now Jesus was doing just that. He was satisfying our hearts, our longings after our son, Andrew. Yet he did infinitely more.

The miracles we experienced could fill pages.

Stephen was expertly cared for at the Manila San and Hospital for forty days. We had pressed our noses against the picture window at the nursery often, greedily watching for every sign of progress. How kind God had been to us. We were learning that this little boy was not a gift to be grasped at, but ours to care for, teach and give back to God. Just before Christmas we brought him home, still a tiny baby, weighing just five pounds one ounce. What rejoicing!

Just as Lionel Whiston had promised us less than a year before, God was using the gift of our two children to teach us more about himself. He had done it through the whole process of pregnancy, labor and birth. Now he was continuing through the death of one son and the life of the other.

We had been in the Philippines only four and a half months when the twins were born and Andrew died. During that period we had been hesitant to let our lights shine in our international scientific community. With Andrew's death we knew we couldn't be "closet Christians" in our professional associations, until then an attractive temptation. We had to pass through the bitter valley of the shadow of death holding tightly to the hand of the Good Shepherd. The death of our son forced us to be who we were.

Andrew's death had a sobering effect on many of our new acquaintances in the international community. We discovered that God wants to use both life and death to draw others to himself. Sometimes he can do that more effectively through death than through life. He is a sovereign God. It is his choice to choose which he will use.

I marveled at his economy in giving us identical twin sons. He chose Andrew to teach us and many of our friends about himself immediately, but left Stephen for us to raise and enjoy. He made them identical so that in my mother-heart I would not have to wonder what Andrew would have looked like if he had lived! I have only to look at Stephen to know.

Death breaks down walls. In our case the wall of cultural differences came down immediately with Andrew's death. As rich westerners we had appeared so self-sufficient and self-contained. Our Filipino brothers and sisters expressed God's love as they cared for us and comforted us in our grief. We learned to receive from them.

Now, years later, often at bedtime a sturdy, inquisitive redhead snuggles into my arms after storytime and asks, "Please, Mommy, tell me about my brother, Andrew, in heaven with Jesus." And I retell him the story of their births.

Often enough Stephen concludes longingly with ". . . and when Jesus comes back to earth again to get us and take us to heaven, then I'll see my brother Andrew!"

Yes, Son, we hope you will. How grateful we are that the death of your brother has helped instill in your mind a longing for Jesus' return.

2

Leaving
Father
and
Mother

The year before we left for the Philippines, we thought that leaving our families and Canada wouldn't be much of an emotional hassle. Going abroad to work was nothing new in either of our families. That year, in fact, Mark's family was spread over four continents.

We knew we would miss our Christian friends from the Macdonald College community at McGill University, especially those in the Sunday Night Bible Study Group. They had stood by us through thick and thin. One member had given us regular financial help so that instead of having to teach I could be Mark's research assistant and typist. The group had encouraged us and prayed us through decision after decision, month after month.

That last year of thesis writing was difficult. Mark worked nights rather than days when the lab was quieter. He gave up all outside responsibilities with the Inter-Varsity Christian Fellowship (IVCF) group and the church we attended. The only thing left on his calendar was the Sunday Night Group. That had to stay. He needed those brothers and sisters.

The last six months before leaving Quebec we lived in the guest suite in the Women's Residence, with more students than ever before flowing through our lives. Some were brand-new Christians, others more mature. Many were excited about the Holy Spirit's activity in their lives. Some came for counseling, others came to counsel me. Quiet times and small group Bible studies were relevant and applicable to everyday life. Life was full.

Getting the job in the Philippines, completion of Mark's thesis, the joy-filled anticipation of the birth of our first child —as well as the actual mechanics of packing and moving—all were surrounded with many evidences that we had found God's will for our lives. No doubts. Just bright green lights saying Go.

Six months later everything had changed. The first morning after our arrival overseas we discovered the packaged breakfast cereal riddled with flour beetles. Ants munched their way into the bread we expected to have for toast. Cockroaches skittered across the bathroom floor when Mark turned on the light during the night. My entomologist husband was unnerved. He confided later that if there had been a plane back to Canada that morning, we would have been on it.

Nothing tasted like home. The pineapple vinegar stung my nose and eyes. The bread, too sweet and yellow-colored, had a sawdusty texture if kept more than a few days—that is, if the feathery, blue mold hadn't nestled into it before then.

One morning, when little white maggots wriggled through the papaya I had planned to serve for breakfast, I was undone. I rushed back up to our bedroom where the air conditioner was going full blast, flung myself onto the bed and broke into convulsive sobs. Mark threw down his shaver and rushed out of the bathroom to me. The shaver buzzed on.

"What's wrong? What's wrong, Wifey? Tell me! Tell me!"

What was there to tell? Surely the facts that there were worms in the papaya, the eggs tasted strange and strong, and the bread turned into a lump of wallpaper paste when you chewed it weren't adequate reasons for my torrent of tears.

Mark held me tightly in his arms and patted me gently, murmuring over and over again, "It's all right. It will all be all right, Wifey." He sounded as if he was trying to convince himself as well as me. We both wondered to ourselves if my emotional outburst was due to the fact that I was pregnant. We did know that everything was strange, unnerving and uncomfortable.

The master bedroom air conditioner roared at its coldest setting. The Venetian blinds were closed tight, the heavy cotton damask drapes drawn shut. Every effort had to be made to keep out the tropical sun. In the mornings when we opened the heavy Philippine mahogany bedroom door, it was like opening an oven full of steaming puddings on a hot summer day. Perspiration would drip from my face and neck before I reached the stairwell. I would grip the banister as dizziness and nausea swept over me, carefully inching my way down the long flight of slippery, polished wooden steps. When I got to the bottom, I reached for the control of the ceiling fans, and turned it to high. I sank into a cushioned rattan chair, waiting for the dizziness to subside. When it did, I moved slowly toward the kitchen, dreading the thought of cooking.

Cooking had been one of the joys of living for me. It frightened me to think that I might have lost that joy in this new place. I mixed the pancake batter methodically. How would pancakes taste without Quebec maple syrup anyway? Perspiration dripped from my forehead into the batter as I stirred. It trickled between my shoulder blades as I fried the cakes. By the time I had made enough for our breakfast, I was ready to retreat back to the shower and the cool bedroom upstairs.

Mark was understanding. "Don't worry about cooking and housework. We can eat at the guesthouse. Just stay in the bedroom and rest and read. I'll come home as fast as I can."

I tried to obey him, but it was difficult.

The laundry pile grew at an alarming rate. The stale smell of perspiration-soaked clothes wafted out of the laundry bin each time I opened it. The house smelled of mildew and dust. Worse than cooking was washing the dishes. If it wasn't done immediately, long lines of ants, tiny black ones as well as big brown ones, scurried out of the woodwork to feast on the batter sticking to mixing bowls or on any tidbits left on the dinner plates. Mark tried to help, suggesting that we could spray insecticide around the kitchen. Of course, being an ecologist he worried about the residual effects of the chemicals, especially since I was pregnant. It seemed that it would be a continuing problem, with increased dangers, after we had a baby crawling around the house. The best ecological pest control would be supercleanliness and antproof storage of all food. Mark helped me with the first control method. We were immensely grateful that the second one was easy: a teacher in the Sunday Night Group had given us a hundred dollars' worth of Tupperware containers before we left Canada.

Every afternoon for those first weeks, after finishing the lunch dishes I wearily pulled myself up the long staircase. Then I threw myself across the large bed and tried to sort out the conflicting waves of first impressions that swept over me, threatening to engulf me.

The world outside the gate of our staff-housing compound seemed so foreign, so needy. Even if we gave away every cent of Mark's salary, it seemed, it wouldn't show a bit of difference in the Filipino community out there. They seemed so poor, we so rich. Mustn't they feel jealous and angry over living in their small wooden houses while we lived in such luxury?

I remembered what a Korean graduate student had told me about the American engineers he had worked with in his home country: their highhanded ways and fancy lifestyles. He was the one who did the hard work, but they got all the credit —and all the benefits.

I shrank into myself, clutching my feather pillow. It smelled of mildew. Now I was the despised foreigner. Tears streamed down my face. We were trapped. Where was our dream of working in a developing country and really being useful? Mark had come here to use his training to increase rice production. He would investigate alternative means of controlling the insect pests of rice rather than simply spraying more and more expensive, lethal chemicals, imported at dollar-gobbling prices from western countries. If he could make some breakthroughs in his field, his work would help the small landholding farmers. I knew *his* work could be worthwhile and helpful.

But I felt useless. Guilt overwhelmed me. Guilt that we lived in such a comfortable house with all the American appliances to make housekeeping easy. More guilt because I found it nearly impossible to keep food on the table and clean clothes on us, never mind ironed ones. Tears of self-pity and homesickness dripped down my cheeks. I pounded the mattress in anger and frustration.

"It isn't fair! It just isn't fair!" I railed. Here we had come to Asia to be helpful and to identify with the people, and all I could do was barely exist. And Mark had to spend so much time comforting me.

For almost six weeks after we arrived, I spent each afternoon on my rumpled bed, weeping and then fitfully napping. I marveled that missionaries could ever get Christian work done in such a debilitating climate. When I prayed for them, I prayed that they could all have air conditioners. I hated myself for being so miserably depressed in the heat, but I felt guilty when I found relief in the air-conditioned room. I was depressed when I used it and depressed when I didn't.

Shortly after five each afternoon, Mark would tiptoe into the darkened room and gently waken me.

"Wifey," he would whisper, "can you wake up? We have an invitation to dinner at seven tonight, don't we?"

"Yes," I would mumble sleepily. "But do I *have* to go?"

For me, there was a definite love-hate element in the invitations with which our hospitality-conscious neighbors inundated us. I looked forward to going because I wouldn't have to go through the agony of cooking our supper, and Mark would get a good meal. At the same time I hated myself that I found it so hard to cook. And then there were the neighbors themselves.

They seemed to be so well read, so sophisticated in their appearance and taste. When they discussed articles in the *Atlantic Monthly* or debated the pros and cons of editorial policy in *Newsweek,* I sat like a stone, finding it difficult to make any intelligent-sounding comments. Their wives were smartly coifed, in well-chosen, perfectly fitted wardrobes. All gourmet, international cooks. How was I going to relate to them as people? Make friends? Share with them the adventures that I had experienced in knowing Jesus? All those adventures seemed very past tense now. Had there ever been adventures? It all seemed impossible. I felt dry, unpolished and very tired.

Although I felt uncomfortable with my neighbors, we did share comparable affluence and foreignness. We came from about eight different countries. I learned, though, that the foreigners had an us-against-the-Filipinos attitude (especially the maids and vendors).

"They're all out to cheat us!" declared one woman. "It's better to buy everything in the supermarkets in Manila. Then you don't have to haggle, and you don't have to wonder if you've been cheated by paying four times the local price." I looked at her silently and wondered if it was really worth driving fifty miles to buy every pineapple and banana one needed. Fortunately, I didn't find my tongue in time and she moved to another topic.

"And don't use the local doctors for more than a cold. Go to Manila and get an American-trained one." She caught her breath and added, "And another thing, smile and greet every maid and gardener you see in the compound. These people are very volatile and if they feel you aren't friendly, they may just stab you in the back some day."

I went home that afternoon confused. I wondered if her descriptive metaphor about Filipino temperament was merely a figure of speech—or if it could literally be true. Some things I had read in North American newspapers before leaving Canada led me to believe that her statement might have some reality to it. It was frightening.

Reading the Filipino newspapers added to my fears. The political situation as revealed by the free press in the early 70s frightened me. Well-schooled in the merits of a democracy, emotionally reinforced by parents who had escaped with their lives from totalitarian regimes, I naturally felt the only God-honoring form of government was an English-style democracy.

When the Americans had replaced the Spanish as the colonial power in the Philippines, they had made great efforts to give the Filipino people opportunities for education (something denied them under the Spanish) and to prepare them for a democratic form of government. Americans benevolently poured money, technology and personnel into that dream, but evidently overlooked two major barriers to its becoming a reality: the centuries-old, patronistic, landholding system and unredeemed human nature.

The Filipinos, a people who place high cultural value on trying to please their superiors, tried to set up a democratic form of government—imitating all the technical aspects, the machinery, of such a form of government. The way it actually worked, however, was not the way the Americans had planned. They had forgotten that in order to make a democracy function, there has to be a large, well-educated middle class to act as a watchdog on elected representatives. In the Philippines there was almost no such class. This was because the feudalistic landholding system concentrated the wealth and power of the islands in the hands of a few families, making up less than ten per cent of the population. Over eighty per cent of the rest of the population was under the thumbs of those landlords. Some landholders employed private armies to convince the people who was boss. Certainly, everyone with vested interests paid politicians to defend their private concerns.

It was common knowledge that many people voted for the politician who gave them the largest bribe. Being a people who love life, especially when speeches and parties are involved, Filipino elections were gala times. They were also violent. Politicians garnered votes while surrounded by burly bodyguards, their weapons barely concealed. The law of the jungle is simple: the strongest and richest gets the game.

Each party had its eloquent, fiery writers in the press corps. Manila's newspapers reported scandal after scandal. Plots were bared. Day after day came intrigue and counterintrigue. When I questioned some of my new Filipino acquaintances about the political turmoils, they merely smiled and shrugged. Their tolerance didn't comfort me. I was more confused and frightened than ever.

We had to live with such fears through years of student unrest, boycotts and barricades. There was no respite until, years later, I realized the source of much of my fears. I had resented the Filipino people for not governing their country exactly as we did ours in Canada. Then I learned to obey the command of 1 Timothy 2:2 to pray for those in positions of political authority over us, and a larger measure of peace came.

In my cool bedroom during those early weeks, in the searing summer of 1970, I tried to assimilate all that was happening to me. Loneliness and confusion strangled me. I sobbed out a prayer: "Lord, whom can I trust? What can I do? Where can I go?"

I didn't want answers. I just wanted to go home.

Gradually I analyzed my dilemma. Mark had meaningful work but I didn't. He felt fulfilled and challenged as he planned his ecological experiments. He had to study the life cycles of the green leafhopper and brown planthopper. He had all the equipment and support staff he needed. A day didn't have enough working hours for him, with so many interesting possibilities to explore. There was so much to learn all at once. Mark loved all the new information and challenge.

My life was so different from his. I longed to be able just to cope. I needed help and advice on how to manage my time in this foreign environment. If only my mother were alive and here now. She would know what to do.

3

The Mistress and the Maid

It was December 1969, six months before we left for the Philippines. Eleanor and I sat at her kitchen table, warming our hands on large pottery mugs filled with steaming Nescafe. Outside, large snowflakes settled lazily on fence posts and rooftops, making St. Anne de Bellevue, the quaint French Canadian town in which we lived, look like a Christmas card. Inside, our animated conversation centered on my forthcoming move to the tropics.

Eleanor and her husband had spent several years in India, where he had been a microbiology professor in a medical college. She was telling me about their experiences, attempting to prepare me for what lay ahead.

"You'll see many things in the Bible in a completely new light when you're in a society where servants are a natural part of the lifestyle," she said thoughtfully. "Jesus said a lot about

servants and masters. So did St. Paul. You'll begin to understand those portions of Scripture as you never have before."

I looked at her, surprised. "I never thought about that
before."

"You'll have to," she replied. "For me, during our time in
India, that area of my life was the one in which I experienced
the most failure, the most guilt, the most frustration. I was so
relieved to get home and run my own house again!" She
paused for a moment, obviously thinking back. "Especially the
cook," she continued. "Shivers still run up and down my spine
when I think about him. I couldn't manage him. He and I
just didn't see eye to eye...."

At that moment Jim, her jovial husband, burst through the
door, saying, "Did I hear you talking about Goh? He was a
great guy! Told the best stories when he went mountain
climbing with me."

I looked from one face to the other. The message wasn't the
same.

"Yes," Eleanor replied, "I must say I hated to be without
you on those expeditions, but I was awfully glad you took him
along."

With that the conversation on servants was dropped and I
rose from the table, ready to leave.

"Oh, one more thing, before you leave," added Eleanor.
"Cultivate your fluency in Low German. You and Mark will be
so glad to have a private language of your own. Especially
when you always have servants around who can understand
every word you say to one another—or misunderstand it! It
will give you some family privacy."

"Thanks," I replied, "I can see how that would be helpful.
I'll try to teach Mark more vocabulary."

That afternoon I walked slowly to our apartment in Married Student Housing, pondering various aspects of our conversation. Questions floated through my mind: What would I
understand better in the Scriptures about servants? Why was
it necessary to have servants in a tropical country? Why had
there been friction between peace-loving Eleanor and her

Indian cook? Should Christians have servants at all? Wasn't it demeaning to a human being to be a servant? I didn't have answers, so I decided to start to search for some. Many of my neighbors were graduate students from foreign countries, so I started asking their opinions.

Daisy from the Caribbean told me that having a housekeeper was the most wonderful gift in the world. When she came down in the morning, breakfast was ready for her. When she came home from teaching school at night, the house was tidy, the table set and the children bathed. Every payday she just handed Emma, the housekeeper, the amount of money needed to run the house, and presto, it ran as smoothly as melted butter.

Flora from South America added that she couldn't be without household help. Physically it was impossible for her to keep up with the amount of laundry necessary in the tropics if one wanted to stay clean. In the rainy season especially, clothing mildewed if it wasn't ironed dry. She added that she was irritated when some of their clothing disappeared, but there wasn't much she could do about it because it was impossible to get along without a laundry woman.

Mira Raj agreed, "Don't trust a one of them. They'll look on you as a rich American—and bye-bye, away your things will go. Lock everything up, including all the kitchen·cupboards."

Their comments and advice left me wondering. Perhaps it would be better to do without help. Surely I could do my own housework.

When I had lived in the Philippines for less than two weeks during the steaming rainy season, however, I began to think differently about household help. With the increase in the debilitating heat and humidity, my energy level sank. Two complete changes of clothing a day were a social necessity.

The frozen and canned fruits and vegetables, mixes and other convenience foods I had relied on so heavily in Canada were unavailable in the Filipino market. Vegetables, fruits, meats and eggs had to be bargained for—each item separately.

Then one had to hurry home and wash everything carefully to prevent spoilage. The whole tedious process took its toll in emotional as well as physical energy.

My mildewy, dusty, insect-infested house began to get me down. Especially after I was invited to share a cup of coffee with a Filipino neighbor. I was met at the door by a smiling little maid, carrying a tray of neatly folded laundry, who then seated me politely and immediately called to her companion to bring snacks. Soon another maid appeared bringing a perfectly laid tea tray, complete with warm Danish pastries. Later I asked my Filipino hostess for advice on the "maid situation." She looked at me levelly and said, "Just don't spoil them. You Americans spoil your girls. They become bad—and opportunistic and greedy because you give them too much. Don't let them go out at night. Be strict."

"Oh dear!" I thought. "I don't want *that* to happen to anyone I hire."

In the meantime I discussed the question with our missionary friends, the Lockharts. First, John advised deciding who is going to be the mistress, you or the maid. Many foreigners in a host country for only a short period want to have a vacation for the entire time. They let servants take over running the house and caring for the children, so they can do their own thing. Some think such an arrangement is great. Others regret the decision after a while, but find it too late to change things without a lot of emotional turmoil—especially in getting rid of one group of servants and training new ones. So they continue to live as "paying guests" in their own homes, annoyed at their servants but unwilling to do without them. The servants usually develop an arrogant manner and disrespectful attitude toward their employers. Each ends up resenting the other's position.

"What an ugly mess," I thought to myself. "I don't want that to happen in our home. We're going to be here for quite a few years." With that in mind, a principle emerged. If we were going to employ servants we still wanted to live as normally as possible. I would continue to manage our home and care for the children. Our servants would be my helpers.

However, my personal dilemma about servants still wasn't solved. I disliked the concept of one person being the mistress and another the maid just because one had the money and the other didn't. I felt uncomfortable and embarrassed about assigning to someone else the housework I had always been able to do myself. Yet during those early weeks, it was clear that I couldn't manage to keep our house clean, let alone attractive, and my husband fed, doing everything alone. Besides, there would be no time for ministering to the people around me.

Then an American neighbor threw a new light on my dismal situation. She reminded me that by hiring someone and paying them generously by local standards, I was not only giving employment and training to the girl but I was also helping her whole family. My neighbor suggested that I hire the girl who was working for her who wanted to study in a secretarial school. Helping a student go to school, while she earned her board, room and partial expenses by doing a few hours of housework a day, would benefit both of us. I was finally at peace with my decision.

However, because of my ignorance of Filipino school systems and culture, I seemed to do everything wrong. Thinking that Filipino secretarial schools were similar to Canadian ones, I thought my student helper would have to go to school for only four hours or so to do her typing and shorthand. Then she would promptly return to wash the day's accumulated dishes.

I produced a set of "Commandments for My Maid" outdoing the Ten original ones in their strictness. When something wasn't done to my liking, I communicated it to her by note. That was a hard, cruel thing to do in a culture where smiling, face-to-face relationships and gentle, oblique personal reprimands are highly valued. There was much miscommunication between us. She responded by pouting. I was galled by the disappearance of little things; she, by my strictness compared with her previous American employer. Besides that, she had the tension of carrying a ten-course load, over half of which were academic subjects that her previous education had ill-prepared her to tackle. Basically, the root problem in that unhappy situation was my resentment of her needed presence in my home. She could accomplish more in her three hours daily than I had been able to do in a whole day. But I was, at that time, unable to recognize my own sin.

Another thing I resented was her observing with eagle eyes, everything I did. Listening to everything I said to Mark or our guests. Commenting in an innocent yet annoying way on how much money I spent on groceries. Asking in a way culturally unacceptable to me how much I had paid for my dresses or dishes. Gossiping joyously with the gardener about everything that went on in our household. Suddenly it seemed we had no secrets. The activities in our home became entertainment for the neighborhood.

My ego, overlarge and very private, rebelled. I hated being in that kind of public eye. Several years later the Holy Spirit brought me to a more humble position. Then I could see (in Philippians 2) that Jesus had not clung to his rights. But not until I chose to give up my "right" to privacy could I be released from the viselike grip of resentment. When the jaws of that vise parted, I was free to laugh at a perfectly obvious fact: our everyday activities, with our particular peculiarities, provided a never-ending source of entertainment for our maids, their friends and relatives. I could see how the shoe would fit on the other foot: if I were living in one of *their* homes, the way they did things would be a constant source of fascination —and perhaps even irritation for me as well.

We were grateful for my friend Eleanor's advice that a second language, unknown to people in our host country, would be an advantage. In some situations it was best for the people around us not to know the content of our conversation. And often it was emotionally freeing to carry on a conversation about intimate family problems without the worry of being understood or misunderstood. When bargaining in the market, we had the advantage of being able to decide on the "right price" without the vendor's knowledge.

After two months with our first maid I had a gnawing feeling (which may not have been true) that she wanted to take advantage of me at every turn. I asked her to leave. Emotionally I was relieved, but I wasn't the winner. Sectors of the Filipino neighborhood marked me as the "Stingy Slave Driver" for years afterward.

Something worthwhile did come out of my unhappy initiation, however. I had tried the advice of my friends and neighbors and it had all backfired. So, remembering what Eleanor had told me, I went to the Bible. I started to study the servant/ master passages, to learn to be a "Christian mistress." One principle seemed to emerge for me: the relationship must be good for both servant and master. If it is good only for the master, or good only for the servant, it is not biblical.

At that point Tina, a Filipino Christian, came to my rescue by offering to contact a relative to work for me. The girl had been a student but had failed her courses. Her immediate family was so hurt and angry that they refused to support her any longer. Since she came from a relatively wealthy family, it was a degrading step for her to become a maid when she herself had been served by others all her life. Her aunt wanted me to train her, thinking a Christian employer could reform her from her sin-filled ways. My teacher's ego leapt at the opportunity and I tried hard. At first she did too. At the beginning we had a teacher-pupil relationship, but I came to love her as my little sister.

She had been spoiled as a child. All of her older sisters had thrown to the wind their opportunities of getting an education. So her parents had set their hopes on her. She would be their professional, their nurse. Then she too had failed them. Living in an American Navy-dominated city as a young teenager had opened her eyes early to the rawness (and lucrativeness) of a "swinging" lifestyle. Later, when the academic load at the university was too much for her the temptation to skip classes became overwhelming. The company of equally undisciplined friends plus the allure of all-day movie houses, added up to academic failure, but much success in learning deceitfulness.

For several months things went well with us. I concentrated on teaching her to do housework thoroughly. Her circumstances forced her to comply with my every request. My ego swelled. Surely that was what a good Christian mistress should do: teach and reform her maids. I allowed her to go to choir practice, the young people's meeting and church. While we worked together at home I did a lot of moralizing. She said, "Yes, yes, Ma'am" to everything I said.

After a few months in the "prison" of our environment she remembered the freedom she had enjoyed with her city friends. Her day off each week began to stretch into several days off as she bused into Manila to be with her loose friends. Obedience and acquiescence disappeared; rebellion and arrogance appeared, breaking my heart.

Finally her mother, relenting, came and took her back home to a distant island, far removed from the temptations of Manila. I was heartbroken, probably more by my own failure to transform her than by the ravages that her willful disobedience to God were already working on her personality.

Tina felt as bad as I did about the whole situation. She felt she had gotten me into it in the first place. In an effort to help she gave me her own maid: a *provinciana,* a country girl with a warm heart but lacking in social finesse. She was a new Christian, eager to learn in every area of her life. I started eagerly to teach her. Her loud laughter bounced off the walls, the dishes bounced out of her hands and smashed to smithereens on the stone kitchen floor. It wasn't easy, however, to teach her the intricacies of American housecleaning or how to make a three-point flower arrangement. But it didn't matter. The sunshiny atmosphere in our home didn't show the dirt in the corners. I learned to love her, and she loved me. She was fiercely loyal and worked tirelessly to please me.

Her clumsiness, however, especially with her hands, nearly gave me heart failure. When she set a plate on the table it always seemed to bounce before it landed. The formal Russian service which she had to master in order to serve our guests according to the standard in our community was almost her undoing—and mine. Especially the unforgettable night when she was serving a minister of agriculture: the gravy boat almost landed in his lap instead of being placed gently beside his dinner plate.

Yet I had no heart to scold her for carelessness, because I knew she was trying hard. So I finally started to pray for wisdom in training her. It was then that I noticed how stiff her fingers seemed to be. The thought struck me that growing up in an isolated village, doing farm work all her life, her small finger muscles had probably had no chance to be developed. I began to teach her to type. It was agony, because my suspicions proved true. She could hardly bend her fingers, let alone control them well enough to strike the keys correctly. But her perseverance paid off. As her typing improved, so did her handling of the dishes and her serving. We were both elated.

From that experience, a practice in teaching maids emerged. Namely, I would try to teach each girl who worked for me some additional skills to the regular housekeeping procedures. Typing was one skill I could easily teach each one. That was following the biblical principle that the situation should be good for both mistress and maid. It gave my maids more self-esteem as well as a practical skill. I had the joy of knowing I was teaching them something marketable.

In the years that followed, as different girls came and went, I added other skills to the list of things I could teach them. Some were directly related to running our household, such as baking and flower arranging. Others, like making greeting cards, sewing and doll making could be used to augment their salaries (although in the early stages I was the principal consumer of their products). It was a joy to watch them blossom in our mutual learning situation.

Papa John Lockhart, who had urged me to make sure who would be the mistress and who would be the maid, gave me further good advice about salary increases for my girls. He suggested that with every skill learned to my standard and satisfaction, I should give a small raise in salary. Therefore, when the cook learned to make bread, she could expect a small increase in salary.

In the area of teaching food preparation my home economics training was especially useful. I could usually analyze each failure and thereby make a positive learning experience out of it. The girls responded very well to that teaching technique (and to the anticipation of a salary increase). Many eventually surpassed their teacher in the quality of products turned out.

Apart from my moralizing with the girl I had tried to "reform," I hardly even thought about my responsibility for my maids' spiritual growth. Then one night we had as a house guest an Asian scientist who was a Christian believer. He came from a country closed to missionaries. I confided to him that I felt helpless in knowing how to witness to the love of Jesus Christ in my environment. He looked at me thoughtfully and then asked, "Are you teaching your maids about Jesus?"

"No. I . . ."

"You must!" His soft musical voice became emphatic. "That's where you must start. Here in your own house. As you teach them from the Word of God and they observe the godly life you live, they will become believers. Their changed lives will convince their brothers and sisters, and they too will be converted to him. Their parents, aunts and uncles will hear the Good News and see it in changed lives. Even their grandparents will respond." His voice reached a crescendo and stopped. We were both amazed at the vision for evangelism he had portrayed to me.

After he left, I gathered up all my courage and started to have inductive Bible studies with the two girls who worked for me. At the beginning it was socially awkward for all of us, but Jesus began to break down the walls that we had built up. It became an occasion that we all looked forward to. Most precious of all, the vision which had initiated it started to come true. That multiplying effect still continues in the lives of people those young women are touching today.

The Filipino girls who have worked for us have been used by the Holy Spirit to teach us. They have given us insights to our host country's culture we could not have gained so easily elsewhere. Their competent, trustworthy work has freed me to have a more direct Christian ministry in the surrounding community. We have learned to be co-workers together, mistress and maids.

4

Welcome
to
Our
Castle

During most of our married-student days in graduate school in Canada we had lived in second-story apartments in old houses. Whenever a guest arrived, I would call down the long flight of stairs, "Welcome to our castle. The drawbridge is down. Come on up." Taking into account the size and age of the landlord's house, our guests would smile at the castle metaphor.

Since two can't really live as cheaply as one (on one scholarship), I usually had teaching or library jobs. They adequately supplied our needs, graduate-school fashion. Those were years rich in spiritual, intellectual and social learning. I learned much about practicing biblical hospitality.

The first year of being a wife is rough, no matter what the books say. Nothing was easy. Mark's thesis was never quite perfect enough for his demanding professor. Besides that, we were living in a different Canadian province, far away from relatives and old friends. And, although I was trained to teach high-school home economics, the school board that hired me assigned me to an elementary school. Looking over my previous teaching experience, the principal decided I was just the person to take on an experimental group of gifted seven-year-olds, mostly from upper-middle-class homes.

Before marriage Mark and I had dreamed beautiful daydreams of having an open, hospitable home. We wanted our home to be open to the needs of university students, especially foreign ones. Once we had that home, however, we also had the demands of Mark's thesis and my lesson plans, and housekeeping. We had almost no emotional or physical energy left to befriend even a few students, let alone to open our door to anyone else they might like to bring along. We had a guest room, even two, if needed, but the beds in them were piled high with unironed clothes, the desks with Think-and-Do Books waiting to be corrected. It was agony and frustration for us. Didn't God call us to be hospitable? Wasn't hospitality a gift of the Holy Spirit that each Christian should exercise?

It was an economic necessity that I teach. Although my class of second graders was made up of smart little kids reading at advanced levels, they were still seven-year-olds emotionally. If I didn't think carefully through my directions to them, chaos resulted. They often looked at their new teacher from the western prairies in bewilderment when she used words and phrases they had never heard before. Keeping those little people profitably occupied learning something new demanded hours of after-school preparation each day. The grade-two curriculum wasn't much help as a guideline. My pupils had already learned everything on it for the year. So, new curricula had to be developed, along with teaching aids and illustrative materials. Consequently, our accumulated dirty dishes often sat in the large old-fashioned kitchen sink for three days before I could wash them. School preparation had to come first. I was driven as much by fear as by professional competence. My principal was anxious to see if giving that select group of students to me had been a wise choice. His crepe-soled shoes made his entering my classroom quieter than the proverbial mouse. He would creep in and watch for a while, and often unsmilingly ask to see my daily and weekly plan books. Consequently, my Saturdays and Sundays largely went into planning the next week's schoolwork. There was no time or energy to clean house for ourselves much less for guests. What made it worse, during that entire time I was plagued with a recurring infection, which also took its toll on my physical energy.

Up the hill from us lived the university's German professor, his vivacious German-born wife and four energetic children (all under eight). They were a Christian family who had recently taken this teaching position in order to be "light" and "yeast" in the university as opportunities opened up.

During that year the secretary at my school was often intrigued by the friendly voice with a strong Bavarian accent saying on the telephone, "Hello? Could you take a message for Mrs. Klaasen, please?" The message was always the same: "Dinner will be served at seven. See you then. Ingrid."

Every afternoon, after the last scarf had been tied and the last stray mitten found, I would drag down to the school office to check my mailbox. Imagine my delight whenever I found an unexpected invitation to supper at the professor's home. The procedure that followed became almost routine. I would phone Ingrid and politely protest that we couldn't come again. (After all, we had just been there a few days previously.)

She, however, would never take no for an answer. "It's a sin to eat a roast alone!" she would declare, and gently go on, "See you at seven, *bitte?*"

I was charmed into accepting her godly hospitality. She never made me feel ashamed that I couldn't reciprocate. I so desperately needed the advice and support of an older Christian woman. She gave what I needed, gladly, generously.

There would be a new spring in my step as I returned to my classroom. Her invitation had freed me from several hours of planning, cooking and dishwashing that day. But best of all were her care and encouragement. With renewed zest I attacked the piles of workbooks to be corrected.

Promptly at seven we would give the brass knocker on the old oak door of their home one thud. The professor would appear immediately.

"Come in, come in, dears!" he would say. "Has it been a rough day? Please come in here and sit by the fire for a moment."

As he took our coats and hung them, Ingrid would fly out of the kitchen engulfed in a huge white apron, looking like a sheet billowing on a clothesline. "Welcome! Welcome!" she would always call gaily, "I'll just be a moment more, yes? Please sit down with my *Schatz* (sweetheart) by the fire." Still waving a wooden spoon in one hand, she would disappear into the kitchen.

The cheery fire and the genuine warmth of Jonathan's caring questions shut out the dismal drizzle outside and the demands of our work worlds. We knew we could always tell Jon the unvarnished truth about our work progress, knowing that he took such things only to the Lord.

True to her word, Ingrid would soon appear at the living room door, announcing, "Dinner is served. Please come to the dining room now."

The professor would rise immediately, adjust the stereo so that the music could be heard in the dining room and escort us there.

In a minute we were seated around the small round table spread with a roughly textured linen cloth. A fat candle, surrounded by a few brightly colored maple leaves, completed the centerpiece. Heavy old silver and a crystal goblet marked each place setting. We joined hands around the table while Jon thanked God for the opportunity to share the meal and time with us. We affirmed his prayer with our own gratitude.

The small roast was deftly carved and placed on our warm Rosenthal plates. A roasted potato and some baked acorn squash accompanied the beef.

Often as not, the Beethoven concerto and the candlelit meal

were interrupted by the patter of small feet on the stairs. A wee voice called hesitantly, *"Bitte, wasser?"* Sometimes it was accompanied by a wet-diaper cry from the baby. Those needs were attended to calmly by the parents, and then conversations were picked up where they had left off.

After the last crumb of apple cake had vanished from the dessert plates and the last drop of tea had been drained, our hostess would gently but firmly ask us to leave. How grateful we were for her insight into our needs. She knew how many lesson plans still had to be completed before I could call it a day.

We had only one brief year in which to learn hospitality from Jon and Ingrid. When Mark's master's thesis was completed and successfully defended, Jon and Ingrid called together some of the Christians associated with IVCF in that city to say Godspeed to us. As a farewell gift they gave us a hand-crafted pottery lamp, reminding us to be "light" in the university where Mark would pursue his doctoral studies.

A few weeks later our old Chevy, hauling all our earthly possessions in a U-Haul trailer, pulled into a small French Canadian town on the tip of Montreal Island. We gaped at the university campus that would be our new home. Its quaint brick buildings with their orange tile roofs, set among giant oaks and flowering shrubs on manicured lawns sloping down to the St. Lawrence River, made us rub our eyes in wonder. Was all that beauty for real? Or were we stepping into the pages of a child's storybook?

In storybook fashion, almost, the Lord worked a series of miracles for us. First, on that very day we were able to rent the upper half of an old duplex on Rue Ste. Anne, and at a reasonable rent. It was unfurnished and curtainless, but we were undaunted and excited to be making a new start. We set up our two folding lawnchairs in the living room, hung beach towels over the windows for curtains and started to invite the people we met into our "castle." This time we wanted to use every opportunity to be hospitable. The Bible taught it, and Ingrid and Jon had practiced it joyfully, in spite of the cost.

Her phrase, "It's a sin to eat a roast alone," rang in my ears. I started to apply it to a pot of curried chicken or a spaghetti casserole. It didn't really matter what you had to share, but how you shared it.

I determined in the second year of our marriage to have the open home we had dreamed so long of having. Being in better physical health and having a nine-to-five job in the university library were definite assets in sharing our home and table more freely. Since the university had a ten per cent foreign-student population, there were many students who valued invitations to our home. They enriched our lives with their experiences, and they added to my culinary repertoire by teaching me to cook dishes from their backgrounds. It was great fun. I learned to decorate birthday cakes with Chinese characters, cook vegetarian curries as well as a meat-and-fish dish from The Gambia.

The handful of Christian students we knew came and brought their friends. One time Mark and I made won ton soup for a Chinese wedding. At one chilly Christmas Carol Sing, they emptied my four-gallon pressure cooker of beef borscht before the evening was over. I don't know if any of the strangers who appeared at our table were ever angels, but I do know that in sharing what we had, we received more than we gave.

On arrival in the Philippines we were excited to discover that we were assigned a three-bedroom duplex. That meant that we could have a permanent guest room. I was delighted when I saw it: Philippine mahogany furniture designed with the clean lines of a Scandinavian export, two large closets, a beautifully caned easy chair, and best of all, a magnificent view. Since our apartment was built on the slope of a defunct volcano, our guest room window looked down over the verdant ravine below, over to the huge flame trees on the opposite bank and beyond to the coconut trees swaying gently at the lakeshore. I was grateful for the special gift of having such an attractive "prophet's chamber" in our new home.

It was fitting that Manuel, an IVCF staff worker, should be

the first to use it. A soft-spoken person of Chinese heritage and a statistician by training, Manny unobtrusively taught us how to welcome Christian Filipino students and their friends into our home. When we needed his help, he was there. He prayed with us about emotional confrontations that upset us. He advised me on how much cloth to give a local dressmaker so she wouldn't be tempted to cheat me out of a substantial remnant. He showed me how to choose high-quality native fruits in the market and how to bargain for them. He even taught our maid how to cook a delectable chicken and chayote dish.

Since there were only two known believers on the university campus adjacent to our housing area at that time, Manny was busy teaching them friendship evangelism. During our first month he asked if he could bring the Christian students and all their contacts to our home one Sunday for supper, singing and conversation. We were delighted. But what would I cook for them? I didn't know how to cook any Filipino food and thought American food would probably be strange and tasteless to them. Finally I compromised and prepared Cantonese-style sweet and sour meatballs, rice, a tossed salad and cookies and ice cream. Students and the Jack Spratts have much in common: they usually lick the platter clean.

After that, whenever the students came, I worked hard on what I could cook for them that they would really like. I wanted them to be fed well and not go away hungry. That was the least I could do for them. I couldn't cook much in the line of Filipino food, yet it was for their dishes that the best ingredients were available in the market. I just didn't know what to do with them. To complicate the issue further, the students came from every ethnic group in the country and all ate differently. One day I was brave enough to share my dilemma with Buena, one of the Christian students. I guess my attempt at ersatz Filipino cooking had been pretty bad that day. She looked at me, smiling, and said, "*Ate* Ruth, when we come to your house, we look forward to having Canadian food. Filipino food we can have any old time. But Canadian food we can have only when we come here." What a relief her advice was to me. After that, cooking for the students was a cinch.

Over the years guests who have stayed in our prophet's chamber have ministered to us as much as we have to them. They have enriched us in amazing ways through their own experiences, giving us an education we could never have had otherwise. Scientists from every continent except Antarctica have stayed in our home. Professional missionaries, Christian student workers, Peace Corps volunteers, tourists and a few of our relatives have come.

My friends sometimes ask me, "How do you do it? How can you manage having so many people come and go all the time?" The answer is simply that I can't do it alone. It's impossible to generate enough physical and emotional energy to minister meaningfully to such a variety of people coming at a fairly regular rate.

First of all, Mark and I agree consistently in prayer that God won't send anyone whom he has not prepared before-hand. God is always faithful to that request, but we sometimes renege on it by not allowing the Holy Spirit to prepare *us.* When we disobey in that basic area, we are soon tempted to feel sorry for ourselves, resenting the amount of time, money and energy one has to give in order to keep one's home open to others. When that happens, the guest, although physically fed, goes away spiritually empty. When we are obedient, we are both fed.

For a professional couple employed by an international agency there is usually another area of hospitality to contend with: entertaining. Because much business is facilitated at social gatherings, and because women have more leisure time and are often lonely for meaningful social contacts, there is much more official entertaining that comes with the job. This type of entertaining is often an unspoken official duty of both the agency's employee and his wife. One can find one's self on a social treadmill, going to cocktail party after cocktail party, formal dinner after formal dinner, many evenings of each week, week after week after week. At the beginning, it's glamorous, exciting, even fun. People on short-term assignments may not tire of the routine at all. For long-termers, it may become a bore. The density of bodies, the noise level and free flow of alcohol make meaningful conversations difficult, though not impossible.

Three days after our arrival we were invited to the home of our director for dinner. I thought I had been bewitched and ended up at Cinderella's ball by mistake. The women wore gold-thread saris and Thai silk gowns. Emeralds, moonstones, cat's eyes and topaz in artistically-crafted gold settings glimmered richly in the candlelight as they held out their perfectly manicured hands to me, the newcomer. Even though I knew the aqua arnel-shantung dress and string of cultured pearls I was wearing looked OK, I felt very much homemade.

We were decorously seated on a patio surrounded by flamboyant flowering shrubbery and lit only by flaming torches and flickering candles. I had no time to collect my thoughts before a white-coated bartender appeared and asked, "What can I bring you, Mrs. Klaasen, a dry martini or Scotch on the rocks?"

I looked up at him, confused, then stammered, "No thanks. Have you got 7-Up?"

He smiled, disappeared and reappeared holding a teak tray with a tall, thin glass of 7-Up on ice, encased in a finely crocheted holder. A neatly pressed hand-embroidered napkin lay beside it.

A young maid right behind him held out a tray of large, succulent shrimp surrounding a zippy dunking sauce. Moments later, another followed with tiny tartlets filled with a crab custard, and another with a tray of sizzling water chestnuts wrapped in bacon. For an hour I watched them come and go, with smiling faces and silent footsteps, bringing more and more drinks and hors d'oeuvres. There were at least eight different canapés and hors d'oeuvres. I had only read about some of the things in exotic foreign cookbooks kept on a special shelf in our university foods lab.

At last, our hostess set her martini glass down and announced gaily, "Dinner is served." And what a dinner it was.

The dining room table was laid with sterling silver and Finnish crystal, framed by eggshell colored linen placemats decorated with cutwork and hand embroidery. The floral centerpiece and matching candles were reflected in the polished mahogany table top. I drank in the beauty of it all. So much better than anything I had seen in *Better Homes and Gardens.*

Our host picked up one of the silver spoons and dug with gusto into the fresh tropical fruit cup before him. I gingerly followed, savoring the hint of mint and honey in the dressing. My spoon was hardly laid on the doily-covered plate, when a white-gloved hand deftly removed it and another placed a warm Limoges plate in front of me. A crisp vegetable salad, arranged to tease the eye as well as the palate, was placed at my left. The waiter whispered, "A roll, Ma'am?" as he offered me a basket filled with tiny, warm croissants, light as a feather. His other hand held out a crystal dish filled with yellow butterballs sitting in a bed of chipped ice and fresh parsley.

We were hardly into the colorful salad when a quartet of maids appeared, led by the cook. Each in turn brought a hot dish, garnished in a china or silver serving dish. There was chicken Kiev, tender beef stroganoff, rice, and then finally, several hot vegetable dishes, prepared to perfection and complemented by smooth, seasoned sauces. The best French restaurants in Old Montreal could hardly compete with this, I told myself.

Dessert arrived, slivers of pie; the filling was layers of French vanilla ice cream interspersed with raspberry preserves, topped with a cloud of beige meringue, still warm from the oven. A rich relative of a baked Alaska, I thought to myself. What a feat to serve it so perfectly on a tropical night.

At some unseen signal our hostess rose and took the women upstairs to her powder room. There we freshened our lipstick, admired her collection of paintings and complimented her on the dinner. When she led us back to the patio, all the tables had been cleared. Only the flowers and candles were left, and a silver coffee service was set on one of them. The bartender was offering a large variety of liqueurs to those who wanted them. Mints were passed with the coffee. Later, another little maid arrived, carrying a trayful of water glasses tinkling with ice. People smiled at one another and made small talk. Eventually the guest of honor and his wife rose. As if at another signal, everyone else rose too, saying their good-nights. At the door, final gratitude for the evening and compliments for the food were extended to our host and hostess.

Mark and I walked down the sloping hill hand in hand, consciously holding back the deluge of first impressions. Suddenly I felt very cold in the tropical heat. "What a lot of work! What a mountain of organization and effort to put in for a night like that! And to think that they don't do it once in awhile, but three or four nights a week!" I was almost totally wiped out by the sophisticated glamour and efficiency that my hostess had displayed. The cook and maids were so perfectly trained the White House would have been happy to hire them. She was my husband's boss's wife. She set the tone and style for all social entertaining in our community. What did that say to me, a newcomer? Too much.

Fortunately, all those years of cooking for large crews of hired men on the home farm now stood me in good stead. My home economics training and joy in cooking would certainly come in handy now. As far as the food preparation was concerned, I thought, with adequate help I could manage. I might have to cook for three days in advance before I was required to give one of those official dinners for visiting scientists and politicians, but that didn't unduly trouble me. Serving alcoholic beverages, however, did.

Having been raised with strong temperance convictions all our lives, and having seen some of the ravages in family life resulting from alcohol abuse, Mark and I were unwilling to serve alcoholic beverages in our home. Someone warned us that our convictions would be misunderstood. People would think of us as cheap rather than virtuous. What is a Christian to do in such a situation when one's convictions collide with the community's social expectations?

About a month after our arrival we noticed from the weekly newsletter that a highly placed administrator, an entomologist by training, was coming through. His name, Hans Pancratz, gave us a hint that he just might have some Russian Mennonites in his family tree. We decided to take a leap of faith and invite him and his family for a small dinner.

I worked diligently on the menu and cooking, including zwieback and *pluma moos* in the list of dishes I prepared. It was a memorable dinner, the very first I would cook for official guests. I didn't know what to expect. My new, inexperienced little maid was even more nervous than I was. She spilled so many things that she washed the kitchen floor three times between five o'clock and the time the guests arrived.

Finally they did arrive. Warm, open-hearted people, sensing our discomfort with our present situation, they did all they could to put us at ease. I served them the papaya punch I had concocted just for this evening and our helper managed to serve the variety of canapés without spilling any of them. Seeing she was too shaky to try to serve our guests using formal Russian service, I set up a buffet instead—and told her to go and read a magazine until I called her. I worried a little about breaking the social standards of our community dinner parties, but there was no choice. Our guests' eyes lit up when they saw the Mennonite food. I had served something like "mother used to make."

After dinner I shared my trepidation about feeling forced into serving alcohol to avoid being misunderstood. My guest, an accomplished hostess with service in many countries, gave me wise advice. "It's true that some people will think of you as cheap just because you don't serve them liquor, but most won't. The strict Hindus and Moslems don't drink alcohol anyway, so you don't have to worry about offending them. What I did when I found myself in the position you're in now, was to spend more time, effort and expense on the meal instead. I made interesting, tasty hors d'oeuvres, used good cuts of meat for the meal and had alternative dishes for the vegetarians. I made my home as attractive as I possibly could. Then I tried to talk to each guest about something that really mattered."

I was grateful for her very practical advice. As I tested it in our home, I found it worked well. I was at peace with myself and with my efforts. And people have not refused to accept our invitations just because we don't serve alcohol.

As far as cooking and menu planning are concerned, I learned to take advantage of my ethnic cooking. Whereas in Canada I had made an effort to cook Chinese, Indian and African dishes for the international students, here I did it only for our own family. Why? Because my Chinese and Indian neighbors who came to our dinners could accurately judge how good the dish from their country really was. That was a disquieting situation for me. It was far more relaxing to cook Mennonite dishes, which they probably never tasted before and maybe never would again.

I also taught our cook how to make one complete American-style company meal, the standard ingredients for which I kept on the pantry shelf and in the freezer at all times. In the event that Mark called me from the office and said he wanted to invite an unexpected guest for dinner that night, I could easily say "Yes." Then, while the cook took care of the dinner, I could continue with the planned activities for that day without much interruption.

The psalmist David has said that the righteous man must be careful when he chooses his servants: "Only those who are truly good shall be my servants. But I will not allow those who deceive and lie to stay in my house" (Ps. 101:6-7). I have thought about that often during these years when I have had to employ household help regularly. Without the help of Christian servants it would be almost impossible to have an open home to the extent that we have now. If they weren't convinced that practicing hospitality was a biblical command, they might resent us and our many guests for their increased workload.

There are a few practical hints I've found helpful in making our household run more smoothly when we have guests. For example, the girl in charge of cleaning the bedrooms and bathrooms has a checklist entitled "How to Prepare the Guest Room and Bath." There are probably fifteen items on that list that she has to see to, from vacuuming the mattresses to placing fresh flowers in the room. Knowing that she will do it competently relieves me of much pressure. A new girl being trained receives a salary increase when she can do this job correctly.

When we have house guests who will stay for an extended period, I arrange for them to have their breakfast separately from our family. That way our morning schedule and theirs don't have to mesh, relieving all of us of that tension. I leave a list of the available breakfast items that our cook can prepare and ask them to tell her directly what they wish to have, where and at what time. For example, although our cook may be able to turn out a perfect cheese omelette, a soft-boiled egg may be beyond her. Therefore, English guests are advised to make their own, if that's what they want.

When we have had a particularly demanding period with much official entertaining as well as personal house guests, I try to give the girls bonus pay for their hard work, and extra time off for rest. I continually praise God for their willingness to obey the biblical command, "If your gift is that of serving others, serve them well" (Rom. 12:7).

Some time ago our Tuesday Group was discussing the apostle Paul's commands about hospitality. Several members had just discovered the Living Bible paraphrase of Romans 12:13: "When God's children are in need, you be the one to help them out. And get into the habit of inviting guests home for dinner or, if they need lodging, for the night."

"Wow," remarked one of the members, "I think it's safer to stick to the King James Version. It's not nearly so easy to understand." Peals of laughter rang through the room as others shared both her sentiment and discomfort at seeing that command so startlingly revealed.

Later, reflecting on what she had said, I thought, "I know just how she feels. It isn't easy to give hospitality, biblical hospitality, which cares most for the guest and not at all for the hostess's ego."

I used to spend hours in anxious preparation, especially for those official dinner parties. Now, I work harder at praying for the people on our guest list, and although the preparation still takes time, the anxiety to impress is drained away, replaced instead with expectation and joy at being able to obey the Lord in this area of our lives. Then our home becomes *L'Abri*, a "shelter" for all who pass through its doors. And God, who gave all, is glorified. What more could a couple ask?

5

Choose:
Priorities
or
Frustration

On arrival in the Philippines, Mark and I had found ourselves in a new world. It was as foreign to me emotionally as it was physically. I viewed everything through the eyes of North American affluence. I was unable to see the people as persons with their own unique cultural characteristics and value systems. Rather, I saw them as "those poor things desperately needing my help."

The comparative poverty of our Filipino acquaintances as well as the country's general economic climate and the chaos and destruction that the wild weather waged on crops depressed me greatly. My goal was to help as many of them as possible. My motivation, however, was not God-given. Basically it was both an attempt to assuage my false guilt and an ego trip. I would be the "Great White Mother" helping all my little brown brothers and sisters. If there was a need I could possibly help with—or if I knew someone who could—I'd jump up and say, "I'll do it!"

Mark, in the meantime, worked smoothly with his supervisor, understanding and appreciating his different cultural mindset. My husband, happy in his work, was content to leave the management of our home and social life to me. He never felt he was working for money; that fact never seemed to occur to him. If I saw needs and if money could meet them, it was fine with him what I did with it.

I was pregnant with our second child. It seemed to me that Mark was consciously or unconsciously putting his work ahead of everything else in life. The world's rice-eating population was mushrooming, and he seemed to feel that it was his job single-handedly to produce more rice. After almost three years, that arrangement was becoming increasingly frustrating and dissatisfying. I resented his devotion to his work. He resented my interference. Hadn't he given me free rein to do what I wanted with my time and the money he earned? Why wasn't I satisfied? Yet he wasn't either.

During homeleave that August we made an effort to visit a pastor in eastern Canada who had often counseled us before. We knew he could be trusted to give sound advice again if we asked. By divinely arranged timing Ron had just been to a management seminar for pastors. Because our toddler needed constant attention, I volunteered to babysit while Mark and Ron talked. I took Stephen out into the kitchen to play with him there, but soon I was listening to what they were saying.

"You have to have a set of priorities for your life," Ron declared. "You can't go on just jumping from one thing to another. Your work is important, but God isn't asking you to wear yourself out physically and emotionally the way you are now. He may want to use you for another fifty years, so don't shortchange him by burning your candle at both ends."

Mark was listening intently to the advice from a godly counselor. Ron continued with some specifics on priorities.

God: You must know him, obey him and enjoy him. **You**

cannot love someone whom you have no time to get to know. Therefore you must make time to enjoy him in private and public worship. You must obey him as he speaks to you through his Word, so that you will experience him actively involved in the humdrum of daily life.

Yourself: Your body is the temple of the Holy Spirit. Take care of it. You must take time to be alone. Enrich your mind. Have hobbies. Enjoy them. Know yourself. What makes you irritable, anxious or frustrated? How can you avoid situations that will precipitate those sins in your life? Know and appreciate yourself as God created you. You cannot love anyone else until you have learned to love yourself.

Your wife: You are commanded in the Scriptures to love her. Make time to get to know her as your friend. Visit together. Take time off for twenty-four-hour mini-vacations together alone—as often as once a month. When you're away from your job, the telephone and the demands of your children, it's so much easier to get to know one another again, to talk about your dreams and goals.

Your children: Take time for them. Time to teach and love them. Time to discipline them so that you can enjoy them and other people won't dread having them about. It's the quality of time you spend with them that counts, not the quantity of time. When you listen to them, listen with both ears—and not from behind the newspaper. Take time to do things with them. Don't worry so much about providing for their future.

Your job: For me as a pastor, people are my work. For you as an entomologist, you have the job of trying to control the insect pests of rice. You must do that work well. It is part of your larger witness—to the other scientists who work with you and the staff that works for you. But don't allow your job to expand to fill all of your time. Ask God for wisdom to allow you to set certain limits to the amount of work you will do—and then do it well.

Ron concluded, "If you follow those priorities in obedience to the Holy Spirit, you'll do a much better job of your work than you are doing now. We pastors were all assured of that at the seminar. I'm beginning to find it true. I know you will too."

Since that conversation I've seen my husband experience many adventures with God as he learned to accept those priorities into his life. But that is his story. I will tell just a part of my own, as I determined to put the same priorities into practice in my own life.

I looked back at our year at Macdonald College, when there had been a constant flow of Christian women through my life and contrasted it with our first year in the Philippines when I had experienced such terrible loneliness. Overseas, I had found no Christian women with whom I could share my turmoils. Mark hadn't understood my feelings: Why couldn't a trip to the hairdresser's, a few new outfits and a bit of extra time to read solve my problems? Wasn't that all I needed in order to relate more easily to the women around me? I tried his suggestions, but they didn't alleviate my sense of inner loneliness and confusion.

Mark sympathized with me and urgently prayed that I find a Christian friend with whom I would feel completely comfortable. The more Mark and I demanded such a friend from God, however, the slower he seemed to be in answering our prayer.

One morning I was sitting at my desk attempting to have a quiet time. Tears of self-pity were rolling down my cheeks as I was singing, "Jesus, I am resting, resting, in the joy of what Thou art," but feeling no joy or rest. All at once, these words seemed audible to me: "My child, am I not enough?" Over and over again the words repeated themselves. I sat transfixed. Ashamed, utterly ashamed. I AM had spoken.

A new relationship began between my Lord and me that morning. Instead of getting my encouragement from other Christians on a regular basis as I had been used to doing in Canada, I had to find encouragement and counsel in the Word of God. I learned to dig. My life depended on it! The Holy Spirit started to make what I studied applicable to my "new" life. I bought a thick notebook and used the Scripture Union inductive study method consistently.

Prayer was hard. Mark and I prayed together audibly at night, but somehow I needed more. If I tried to pray alone, my mind wandered. Finally, I started to write out my prayers in a notebook. That helped. I remembered again what I had been taught in an IVCF group from Rosalind Rinker's books on "faith-sized requests." It had been frightening to realize that my faith wasn't Sanforized. I had watched my faith shrink in the Philippines. What had worked in Canada didn't work here. I had to start all over again, praying for only as much as I could really believe God could do in this foreign environment. Using a notebook helped give me a record of prayer requests and how they were being answered. Patches of joy crept back into my life.

At that time I thought that having regular, effective quiet times and learning how to pray were all I needed to fulfill the priority of putting God first in my life. My attitude toward the denominational church was intensely (most often unjustly) critical. I thought that worship meant attending Sunday morning services, so I did that quite regularly. But if I had what I thought was a legitimate excuse to stay at home, I eagerly took it. My critical spirit kept me from appreciating and learning from the various aspects that made up the morning worship. If the sermon wasn't helpful to me, I considered the whole exercise a waste of time. There seemed to be no relationship between the Sunday service and what I was learning in my quiet time.

Experientially, I recognized that I wasn't an island. I needed and longed for contact with fellow Christians. Therefore, when Filipino Inter-Varsity staff or missionaries would visit our home, I would talk my heart out. My heart was so full of all I was discovering that I had to share it or I thought I'd burst. Then we had not yet learned that, inherent in the first priority of commitment to God is commitment to the body of Christ.

In the set of priorities he gave Mark, Ron had said that we

needed to give ourselves second place—before others. That was new and uncomfortable for me. An acrostic my Sunday-school teachers had used for JOY still stuck fast in my mind. It said J—Jesus should be first, O—Others second, and Y—You last. Ron had quoted to us Jesus' words, "You must love your neighbor as yourself." Further, he had said that we *cannot* love others until we have learned to love and accept ourselves. I already knew that certain schools of psychology emphasized that, but had passed it off as being unchristian.

Some of our Mennonite churches had taught a somewhat lopsided theology which tended to stress human depravity. Phrases like "no good thing can come from me" and "I am a worm" were used by truly humble Christians. In some circles, talking about personal spiritual growth was taboo—but criticizing the preacher's sermons or the work of the deacons wasn't. In other Mennonite circles (there are many different ones under the umbrella called Mennonite), personal conversion was stressed. Older people talked longingly about "just being sure to be able to get over the doorstep into heaven" when they died. They talked quite a lot about the joy they would have in heaven, especially those who had suffered much persecution in eastern European countries and had miraculously escaped to Canada. However, Jesus' blood and righteousness had little effect on their joy in living now. Life, even when it was materially good, was something they complained about. And they tried as much as possible, verbally, to focus away from themselves. The focus instead was on the accomplishments of the children and relatives.

It was a sign of a good, and therefore godly, Mennonite woman to always sacrifice herself for her family. To her, especially in her role as wife and mother, belonged the "left-overs" of time and energy for herself, and of money for clothes or for appliances for the house. That was most graphically seen when our people lived in rural areas. The farmer would have the latest machinery in his yard, his workshop would be well equipped and his spacious barns arranged for maximum efficiency in cattle feeding. His wife was expected to care for the needs of a large and growing family in a tiny, ill-equipped house that might not even have indoor plumbing. A good wife was one who didn't notice such discrepancies, but instead patiently and quietly labored on under the adverse working conditions, which to her were normal. Her goal was to acquire a reputation for being a thrifty, hardworking wife. That was ironically synonymous with godliness. If and when her work was praised, she was to smile and say self-effacingly, "Oh, with me it is nothing."

With that type of conditioning, no wonder I had difficulty with the second priority. (Women coming from a very different background might have to battle with selfishness in the amount of time they spend on themselves.) But in the Philippines, I found myself in a situation a generation and a world removed from the world I had known.

The man I married happened to be a Mennonite Christian. As a poor pastor's son, he had watched how his mother had to scrimp and save to keep her family fed and clothed. She had done it with remarkable skill and verve, but he didn't want his wife to have that same type of life. Consequently, when he started to earn a salary, and the constant pressure to make ends meet was off, he would just bring home the pesos and say, "Here, Wifey, spend all you like. When this is gone, I'll get more."

Because of a lack of priorities in my life, for several years I seesawed between overindulgence in what I spent on myself and self-denial. Either way was unsatisfying because I was left with either a load of guilt as heavy as my purchases, or I felt shoddy in the presence of my friends, ending up despising myself.

When I started to consider the second priority, the easiest place to start was with my personal appearance. At that time it was also the most urgent consideration, because I was uncomfortable in the presence of my well-groomed neighbors. I soon discovered that if my hair was well cut and shampooed, and I was well-groomed, I felt much more relaxed in their presence. Although polyester clothes are hotter than cotton ones, they don't wrinkle, giving a neater overall appearance in the tropical weather. Miniskirts were the vogue then, but I wouldn't wear them; instead I chose pantsuits and floor-length skirts for my wardrobe. At first I resented the new time spent on myself, but I found that when I didn't draw undue attention to myself by being underdressed or over-dressed in the world in which I now lived, I could relax and forget about myself. What a relief.

Neatness and orderliness are two virtues my mother had difficulty teaching me. I discovered, however, when every-thing was messy, I became easily frustrated and irritable. My life definitely ran more smoothly, and I was happier when my house was in order.

Since the maids freed me from the routine of housework, I had blocks of time to spend I had never had before. When-ever Stephen was awake, I proudly spent all his waking min-utes playing with him, trying to stimulate him intellectually, walking him around the neighborhood in his stroller, brag-ging to my neighbors that our maids didn't touch him unless absolutely necessary.

Yet I wasn't finding my emphasis on total motherhood as satisfying as I had been led to believe it would be. That was because I was denying my need for intellectual stimulation and involvement. When the urge to write would come too powerfully to resist, my fingers would fly across the keys until a manuscript was finished. Then I would come away feeling fulfilled and happy, yet a little guilty that I hadn't spent those hours with Stephen. It was false guilt. God had arranged my situation so that I had reliable babysitters right under our roof every day. I finally decided it would be all right to leave Stephen with them sometimes. So I began to feel free to set aside two hours a day to write, and if Stephen wasn't sleeping, one of the girls would take him out to the playground or play with him on the patio. It was a good arrangement for all of us.

The Holy Spirit is patiently but continually showing me areas of my life where I need to change—or where I need to accept myself. Areas such as undisciplined and undirected reading in leisure time; undisciplined overeating when I am tense or emotionally disturbed; a need for at least eight hours of sleep if I am to function effectively the following day.

Because my lifestyle had become so sedentary, my body wasn't getting adequate exercise. We had a large, clean swimming pool in our neighborhood, but I couldn't enjoy it because I'd never learned to swim well. That meant making the socially uncomfortable decision to ask the Filipino lifeguard to teach me how to swim, along with Stephen. It was a difficult undertaking for both of us. But because I was convinced of the necessity of priority number two, I stuck with it.

Now I'm glad I've taken the time to consider this second priority. It is very satisfying for me to realize that God created me with my own special background, family, appearance and intellectual and spiritual gifts. I'm grateful that I'm me, and am no longer berating God for not making me someone different. Instead, I'm rejoicing in new discoveries along the way as I'm learning to be the woman he intended me to be when he created me.

A warning about priority number two should be added here. At the time we received Ron's counsel, it was the first time in our lives that we had been taught self-acceptance. Prior teaching had emphasized self-rejection. Walter Trobisch's book *Love Yourself*, had not yet been published. According to Trobisch, the fact that self-love must precede our ability to love others does not mean, or even imply, that self-love should supersede our love for others. The order in which these priorities are arranged is to emphasize the importance of the "timing" of each of the other priorities. For example, if God has first place in my life, then priority number two follows because I know I am his creation, his child, and I can accept myself as I am. I no longer have to fear getting to know myself, nor can I reject or hate my body, the house of the Holy Spirit, by failing to exercise or by overeating. It follows too, as I am under the lordship of Jesus, that I dare not indulge myself and use priority number two as an excuse to neglect my husband or children.

The arrangement of these priorities emphasizes to evangelical Christians that we learn to appreciate that we are created by a sovereign God, in his own image. When we consciously or unconsciously neglect our bodies and minds, which he specifically created to be used for his glory, we do not honor him.

My husband was to have a definite place: priority number three. When Mark and I were first married, I had put him on a pedestal as my Mennonite background had taught me to do. I smothered him with attention. It was an enviable position for a man when contemplating it from a distance, but a most uncomfortable one when experienced at close range. Fortunately for Mark, I had to teach in those early years, giving him some breathing space.

As time went by, intellectually, and to some extent spiritually, we both went our own ways. He was a "science man," while I was the "arts type." We lived as two compatible roommates bound by mutual respect and a well-adjusted and enjoyable sexual bond. That basic pattern continued after our arrival in the Philippines. Mark became more involved than ever in his work, and I with people. Since there was usually a spiritual dimension in my people involvements, I soon rationalized that it was legitimate to put other people's needs ahead of Mark's. Mark, I reasoned, was so well put together, that he didn't really need me much. I didn't even regularly pray for my husband and his needs. If I had, I wouldn't have known what to pray for, since we so seldom talked alone.

A few times each year our lack of regular communication backfired, resulting in tears and talkathons lasting into the wee hours of the morning. Neither of us consciously wanted to have only sporadic communication, but we didn't know how to change our present dilemma. Ron's list of priorities gave us the key.

I saw that Mark had to have a definite place in my life, a definite time slot, and I a place in his life. The process of becoming friends as well as lovers was initiated again. We started to make dates to get away to Manila without the children for twenty-four-hour mini-vacations in a hotel or guest house. We limited the number of luncheon and dinner invitations we accepted in a week to insure adequate time alone together. Sometimes we even brought lists of things we wanted to talk over with each other on those special dates. We both were alert to opportunities to be together, be it short walks in the moonlight, or a drive after dark around the experimental rice plots. (The highways were too crowded for romantic cruises.)

As we began to make time to talk to one another, our marriage started to grow in exciting new ways we had never experienced before. We were learning to obey the scriptural injunction "to cleave to each other."

The main reason I had time that year to think about the priorities Ron had given us—and time to start putting them into practice — was that my doctor had grounded me. My second pregnancy was difficult. The same old problem: from the beginning of the second trimester my uterus would contract for no apparent reason, signifying to the doctor that the fetus was attempting to abort. Because I was forced to stay close to home, and couldn't take on responsibilities in our church or community, I learned something of the value of following these priorities experientially during the waiting period.

Best of all, Bethany Anne Klaasen was born full term, a cuddly almost eight-pound baby. Since she was the result of consulting fertility specialists and much prayer, delivered by emergency Caesarean section after curfew during a gas-rationing period, her safe arrival was cause for much rejoicing. We were so grateful for both of our children and determined to give them the place in our lives they needed and deserved.

In Charlie Shedd's book *Promises to Peter,* we had learned that the best insurance for children is the husband's love for his wife. Children are never jealous of the love parents have for each other. That love relationship is their best source of security. In light of that, putting one's spouse before the order of priorities, children made good sense to us. Our marriage started with an empty nest and would end with an emptied nest. While the children were in it, however, they had to have definite time and a definite place. Children are aware of their right to their parents' time. They demand it with unacceptable behavior if they can't get adequate amounts of it otherwise. Time with children is best utilized when it is planned and structured.

After reading this book, Mark decided to take two-and-a-half-year-old Stephen out alone for lunch one Saturday each month. After lunch they would go to Mark's lab and field plots. Mark took time to show Stephen the insect damage on rice plants and allowed him to look at insect specimens under the microscope. After returning from the first of those get-togethers, Mark confided to me, "Stephen hardly ate a thing. He just talked one blue streak. He had so much to tell me." That first luncheon was a revealing experience for both Mark and me. I learned how much our little son looked forward to being alone with his father, and Mark learned how much his son had to communicate just to him.

And later, when Bethany turned three, she celebrated her birthday with her first luncheon out with her father. It was an occasion she looked forward to for weeks prior to the actual date. Each time we drove past the Kentucky Fried Chicken outlet, Bethany would point to it and chirp, "I'm going there alone with Daddy when I'm three. Mommy can't come. Stevie can't come. Just Daddy and me."

Some special problems arise when raising children in a cross-cultural or multicultural environment such as ours. Through Ron's teaching we realized that we couldn't just be casual about our children's upbringing, leaving them with nursemaids much of the time while we rushed out to solve the world's problems, whether in food production or in broken relationships. As the old proverb goes, "Our own fences had to be mended if we didn't want our sheep to stray."

I started to keep a Priorities Notebook. Each morning after my quiet time, I would list my priorities for that day, starting with God and then going through each family member, including the servants. At the end would be a category entitled "Others," followed by "Housework." I would think through each child's activities for that day, the friends they might play with, special things we could do together or household activities they might be able to help me with, thereby giving us additional time for conversation. Stephen became so accustomed to having a schedule of activities that sometimes he would come to me and ask, "What's next on my list for today?" But the lists aren't followed legalistically. They act as a guideline. Their value is that they give a sense of direction, a sense of accomplishment and give the family constructive things to do together.

After I learned to write down my priorities and responsibilities in this way, I was freed from much guilt. I knew that I was trying to do things in the order that God would have me do them.

Homemaking took on new meaning and new freedom simultaneously. I didn't have to compete with my neighbors in how well my house was decorated. Our home could reflect us. We could enjoy it with its expanse of garden, but not worship it nor complain about the work and expense involved in its upkeep. But like Mark, I have to set limits on how much time I spend running and decorating our home, and not allow that job to fill up all my available time. That limitation has been relatively easy for two reasons. One is that I enjoy people more than things; the other is that I enjoy setting a reasonable number of goals for each month for what I will do on the house. Those I look forward to doing, if possible, and no more.

It was such a relief to have some guidelines for my life. To find that there was then enough time for other people and for their individual needs was joy indeed.

6

Marriage,
Children,
Families . . .

I had been raised with the notion that husbands, and men in general, were somewhere next to God. Their word was law. Women obeyed them unquestioningly. A henpecked husband in our Mennonite communities was a rare bird. If there was one, he was alternately laughed at and pitied, and his wife was shamed. The Pauline passage in Ephesians 5 about wives obeying their husbands was used as a psychological whip to keep wives in their quiet, subservient places. The companion commands for husbands to love their wives and for believers to submit to one another out of love were largely disregarded—to the grief of many wives.

On Sunday afternoons when the women gathered in grandma's big bedroom, they shared their marital heartaches with one another. If on those occasions an unhappy wife was able to get some emotional support from others, it was also true that the women usually divided themselves into opposing camps, those for her and those against. Sometimes secret information shared from wounded hearts later fueled community gossip. I don't remember the women praying for one another, but probably some of them did, from their beds on sleepless nights after they had been used by insensitive husbands.

As a high-school student, watching marriages was not the preoccupation it had been earlier in my life. I was more interested in dating the handsomest, smartest or most eligible boys in my community. From glimpses into the lives of various couples who were our youth sponsors or teachers, it seemed that some marriages were better than others. I was too busy to analyze why.

As a new Christian and young university student, I had a chance to see some marriage models that impressed me deeply. One was the home of a Mennonite genetics professor. In that home the wife had a place as a person. She was an artist. Her home displayed her workmanship to its best advantage. Her roles as wife and mother were appreciated. The father taught his sons to show their mother gratitude for the work she did in the home, as well as give her the help she needed. The couple respected one another spiritually, intellectually, socially and physically. That is true love.

During a few days' vacation in their home, my eyes didn't miss a detail, my heart drank it all in. I remember standing in the hallway in that home and praying what seemed then an unattainable dream: "Lord Jesus, please give me a husband who is a Christian Mennonite biology professor and let me have a marriage and home like this one."

God is so good! Five years later the fulfillment of that prayer started, when I said a resounding "I do!" to a Christian Mennonite biology graduate student. The adventure of making our marriage grow had begun.

We had a glorious courtship. I was so tremendously grateful that God had not called me to remain single as I had feared he might. I saw in Mark the fulfillment of my earlier dream-prayer. The day came, however, not many months after our magnificent wedding, when I sat in the middle of a room I was trying to rearrange and said, "Is this all there is to it?" I was disappointed. It wasn't as glamorous as the magazine articles had led me to believe. I still got tired, the house got dirty and Mark wanted to read the newspaper at night instead of talk to me.

As I sat in that cluttered second-floor apartment, wondering what had somehow gone amiss, the idea struck me that our relationship had to continue to grow, just as it had up until the wedding day. Somehow I had thought that the wedding day was the culmination of our relationship instead of the initial knot, such as one would tie to begin creating a decorative macramé hanging.

Continuing to build our relationship after the wedding meant planning events to which each of us could look forward. It meant making new friends to whom each of us could relate, as well as giving one another room to cultivate individual friendships. Many of my closest friends are women who are not married. Mark has always encouraged such friendships, and has sometimes given my friends valuable counsel and encouragement from his perspective as a man and a husband. More than that, he has given me freedom to develop correspondence with several older male authors who have made it their special ministry to me, as a fledgling writer, and to us as a couple, to encourage us with their letters and prayers.

Sources of possible tensions and quarrels were minimized since Mark and I are both Christians with similar backgrounds. We have only slight differences in our values and we respect each other and those differences. We want to obey God individually and in our life together.

During the five years Mark was a graduate student, we worked hard at developing a ministry with students in the university, in the high school where I taught and in the church we attended. We moved pretty much as two compatible roommates who came home each evening dog-tired, grateful to cuddle together in one warm bed at night. At student functions we went our own ways. We had seen too many young married couples cling to each other at public meetings as if demonstrating their deep love to the group, who had to watch them uncomfortably. We probably went too far in the opposite direction, failing to provide single students with a sufficiently positive marriage model. Going out alone together seemed a sin when we could be taking a foreign student with us. We didn't know how to spend a quiet evening alone at home, talking about the direction our lives were taking. Instead we had someone over, worked, read or slept.

It was that basic pattern of going our own way that we continued during our early years in the Philippines. New tensions on each of us, however, strained the pattern. It soon became evident that something, or someone, in our marriage would have to change.

Because we came into a new international community where no one knew us and we knew no one, we had only each other to confide in. We were forced to discuss our actions and activities ahead of time. We saw our own cultural values come into confrontation with our host country's values. There was no one to discuss disconcerting situations with, except each other.

The fact that Mark had meaningful work that more than filled his time, and I didn't, became a source of tension between us. During the five previous years of our marriage I had always had work that I found challenging and enjoyable. The things that now filled my time seemed relatively insignificant such as coffee parties, the maid's behavior, problems with dressmakers. Mark tried to be interested, but in the end all he could say was "Wifey, do whatever you think best."

"How am I to know what's best?" I would rail back. "I have no one to talk to about these things but you."

He would sigh and try to listen and give helpful suggestions while I babbled on about the issues of my world. As I listened to myself, I had to admit how insignificant my problems were. But they were real to me. For years he listened to me complain about all the finicky details of household situations I had never had to deal with before. Not until I learned that my constant complaining was sin was Mark released from my tirades.

The temptation to turn to other women was a readily available one. In the Philippines, if a man can't find comfort and warmth at his own hearth, he can easily find it in the arms of a sympathetic filipina. Neatly groomed and dressed becomingly, many look like dolls. Their shy coquettish smiles and natural gracefulness add to their attractiveness. Contrasted with their American and European counterparts, who are sometimes sloppily groomed and dressed, often overweight and loud-mouthed, they may cause lustful temptation for some foreigners.

The attractiveness of Asian women can breed jealousy and suspicion in the mind of American wives. Lack of meaningful work, even the work of running their households, leaves the wives free for a dizzy round of coffee, bridge, cocktail and dinner parties interspersed with golf, tennis or swimming. At each of those activities juicy tidbits of gossip are often exchanged. When one constantly hears what So-and-So's husband has done, one begins to wonder what one's own husband is doing. That atmosphere, rife with intrigue and suspicion, coupled with bitter complaining, eats like acid on the metal of any marriage. I, too, had my fears.

One day I was brave enough to mention some of them to Mark. He gave me a reply that both frightened and comforted me.

It's true, I'm tempted, darling," he admitted gently, "I'm a man, not a stone. Every time a girl in a miniskirt walks by, I have to choose to avert my eyes. Adulterous thoughts want to take root in my mind."

My eyes widened as I searched his serious face. He continued, "The all-important thing you have to pray for, Wifey, is that I'll stay close to God. If I obey him, then you and our marriage will be safe."

"Yes, but . . ." I gulped.

He gathered me into his arms and finished firmly, "You

have to learn to trust God's faithfulness rather than mine. His is utterly reliable."

In the years since, when Mark has had to jet from country to country, fact-finding and giving advice on rice-insect infestations, his words have been rooted in my heart. As I pray for him, praising God for his present love and care for both of us, I am comforted with the quality of peace which passes all understanding described in Philippians 4:7.

Tangible evidences of my love are packed in his suitcase in the form of notes, written in advance for each day he will be away, telling of activities that the children, friends and I will be doing; favorite snacks or some new books to read during the long evenings alone in a strange hotel room.

We've both come to appreciate, however, the aspects of our present situation that have a positive effect on our marriage. Because I've had servants while our children are small, I haven't had to battle the constant weariness that plagues most wives with preschool children. I could nap in the morning after being up all night with a fretful baby. I didn't have to struggle with excessive attacks of postnatal blues. The baby was ours to enjoy without the dirty diapers. The maids took care of the laundry. What bliss.

Then there were all those handyman jobs about which most North American wives regularly nag their husbands. I didn't have to worry Mark about them. Gardeners, plumbers or carpenters took care of them instead. That reduced a whole area of potential tension in our marriage.

The blocks of free time I had never had before, I could use as I chose: shopping, studying, reading or socializing. It was my responsibility to plan that time well so that it could be enriching. In the early months of our first year in the Philippines I read as much Filipino history and literature as I could. Some of it I wish I had shared with Mark, by reading it together or summarizing a book for him after I'd finished it. That is a goal I have for enriching our marriage in the future.

On looking back, in spite of all our muddling, I see that God has held our marriage together. We wanted to do his will. He started to teach us what it meant to "cleave to each other and become one flesh" as the Word instructs us to do. The "one flesh" principle encompasses so much more than learning to be compatible lovers.

Becoming one flesh means learning to understand the psychological makeup of the other partner, their strengths and weaknesses. It means not expecting more than experience has taught you they can give. It means learning to appreciate the other person for exactly what they are now, not what they may or may not become. It means soothing their emotional hurts, just as one would care for a cut on one's own physical body. It means sharing goals, dreams, hopes and fears. But it takes time for a marriage to mature so that the partners are secure enough to open themselves to one another emotionally.

Making time alone started slowly. It was far more difficult than we thought it would be to leave our children with someone else while we drove in to Manila for a day alone together. Having each meal at a different restaurant, and walking together, we started talking about all that was happening to us individually and as a family. At first it was strangely uncomfortable. We weren't used to having uninterrupted conversations with one another. We don't succeed in "taking a vacation" every month, but we have a tremendous incentive to try because of the enrichment it brings to our friendship as a couple. In California on sabbatical leave we found it difficult to get away overnight, but tried to go out for lunch one day each week instead. Sometimes we packed a picnic and sat on the grass in a nearby park for that hour. The result was that we always came away refreshed and encouraged—and grateful that God ordained the institution called marriage.

In a marriage it is usually the "little foxes that spoil the vines." That took me a long time to realize. I would put Mark's requests and needs behind those of others, thinking erroneously that such was God's will. Little requests like "Could you buy some transistor batteries?" or "Could you set over the top button on this shirt, so I can wear it with a tie?" were easily forgotten. If I felt Mark was neglecting *me,* he soon heard about it, yet I consistently neglected him and expected him to be consistently forgiving and patient. Later, when I set up my Priorities Notebook, under Mark's name I disciplined myself to write down his requests immediately rather than say, "Yes, I'll do it," and then let the request fly in one ear and out the other.

I had to learn to accept Mark and his poor estimations of how long it would take to finish a paper he was writing. Mark works well under pressure, I don't. Several times a year he has major papers to write and present. He likes to get all his material together and then work at it day and night, concentrating all his energies on the project at hand. I've had to learn that to love him at those times is to shield him from unnecessary visitors, social engagements and household problems. When he says, "I'll finish this by the 12th, at the latest," I suspect that he's overoptimistic and that it will likely take until the 15th. To avoid disappointment and unnecessary emotional confrontation, I just make a mental note of the date I think he will actually finish, based on past experiences. During such periods I often write in the Priorities Notebook under Mark's name "Allow him to work." That is a gift I can choose to give him or choose to withhold. To withhold it is to load him with the additional burden that he is working late again without my approval.

When I first started to consciously consider Mark as having third priority in my life, I would list under his name in my notebook such things as "bake him a lemon meringue pie," or "buy a birthday card for him to send his mother." Now added to the above, might be a quotation from a book I want to discuss with him, a call to someone for information he needs for a Bible study he's leading, or special prayer throughout a day that looks bleak for him from the beginning. Some nights I deliberately feed the children early and put them to bed so that he and I can have dinner and time to talk.

A new sense of obedience and emotional release enters my life as I give Mark a definite, rightful place in my conscious planning for a particular day. I'm learning to appreciate his personhood with the abilities and inabilities, maturities and immaturities, he possesses—always aware that we complement and complete each other as we are being molded into the oneness God intended us to have when he gave us as gifts to one another.

In *I Married You,* Walter Trobisch expounds what happens when a couple "leave father and mother, cleave to each other and become one flesh." Trobisch's book has amazing power to communicate its message to people from various cultural backgrounds. In it, he describes asking an African audience what came after the word "flesh" in their Bibles. They were puzzled for a while, until one bright young fellow yelled, "Full stop!" In North America we would have answered, "A period."

Thus Trobisch wisely pointed out that God didn't say that a marriage had to have children to be complete—a shocking revelation to an African mind. Children are an added blessing to a marriage, not a necessary ingredient. Yet the Bible does say that they are a tremendous blessing. God can teach a couple with children things that are difficult to teach a childless couple. So many metaphors in the Bible speak of both the fatherhood and motherhood of God. We understood them in an entirely new light when we became parents ourselves.

Children need to be taught that they are a blessing, a gift. Many parents make too much of the bother, expense and responsibility that their children are to them. Or they may overindulge their children, shielding them from the harsh realities of the world.

The Bible makes clear that parents are to teach their children and discipline them. Those are difficult and time-consuming commands for Christian parents to obey. The training of children cannot be left to the school, not even a Christian school. Nor can it be left to the church because their exposure would be a meager Sunday teaching. The social environment in which most believers find themselves, whether in North America or abroad, is basically post-Christian or anti-Christian. We must consciously accept the responsibility

to teach our children what God's Word teaches and be alert
to share with them evidences of God's power in daily life as
they occur. As we give God first and overall priority in our
lives, evidences of his love will appear. Our children will learn
to watch for them, and rejoice with us.

If you want to learn what goes on in the imagination of your
children, start to play with them regularly. While playing with
parents, children learn how to lose gracefully, cooperate and
be considerate. When setting priorities for the day, I try to
set aside time to play with each child specifically for at least
twenty minutes. It has to be scheduled; otherwise time alone
with a child becomes as elusive as catching a shadow. When I
started to give my children full attention for periods of each
day instead of halfhearted attention all day long, their fuss-
ing and whining decreased.

Living in a cross-cultural environment, children quickly become aware of the differences. Because people from different
countries often have different outlooks on life, values and
ideas of discipline, the route of least resistance is to get to
know people from your own country and not bother about the
rest. However, that is an impoverishing position for a parent
to take. If one wants one's children to gain the advantages
of growing up in a cross-cultural situation, one must make
efforts to arrange learning situations for them. They must not
be allowed to entertain the false supposition that to be different means to be inferior. We found that differences in food
preparation, ways of eating or levels of cleanliness explained
to our children at a young age were accepted as natural in the
course of events, and with a minimum of fuss. We arranged
play times with the children of Filipino believers who didn't
live in our immediate neighborhood. Within our neighborhood, I encouraged Stephen to play with children from other
countries as well as with Americans. That meant setting up
appointments by telephone and sometimes entertaining the
mother so that the children could play together. As a result,
our son has learned to enjoy the Japanese art of paper folding,
and munches a *chapati* (Indian bread) or a *suman* (Filipino rice

stick) as willingly as a chocolate chip cookie.

Teaching the value and dignity of work is particularly difficult in a family setting where servants are part of the lifestyle. It takes much discipline on the part of parents to keep children doing work assigned to them, instead of letting the servants do it for them. We started to assign Stephen small jobs from the time he was four. It was absolutely taboo for a servant to help him. He received a certain amount of money for each job performed cheerfully. If it was done grumblingly, payment was withheld. That started to teach him the value of working gladly, as well as the fact that one has to work to earn the things one wants.

Among American families, especially those living abroad, there is a tendency to give children everything they want. The parents themselves may feel a false sense of deprivation from living abroad. Feeling that their child is missing so much by not being able to play in the Little League or eat MacDonald hamburgers, they tend to compensate for such supposed losses with material things. They make the mistake of giving them things rather than their time.

One great deficiency for children growing up abroad is their lack of knowing their own extended families well.

God had a special way of meeting this need for a family for us while we were abroad. Five years before we even dreamed we would work in the Philippines, I had met an English missionary, John Lockhart, at an IVCF-sponsored missions seminar at my university. In the Philippines he produced and published Christian literature. As I listened to him I became excited about his work. But that year I had very little money, and wasn't about to part with the ten dollars I had in my purse to support it. That money was a gift from a physically handicapped Christian teacher. Her note accompanying the check had read: "Because you've chosen to 'mother' your orphaned younger brothers and sisters this year, rather than teach, I'm sending you this money from my first paycheck for you to buy something for your trousseau."

At the end of that seminar, I found myself propelled to the

lectern, saying, "Sir, here is ten dollars. Five of it is for literature work in the Philippines. The other five I want you to use
to buy something special for your wife, some flowers or something else she would enjoy."

Mr. Lockhart's eyes twinkled as he thanked me. "There's
nothing I'd like to do more than obey your instructions to the
letter," he said.

I went home with a heart as light as my purse. Joy-filled at
my unexpected obedience, I thought no more about it until
Mrs. Lockhart's thank-you note arrived. It was such a delight-
ful letter that I wrote her another in reply. Our correspondence continued for five years. Only after we had been in the
Philippines several weeks did I meet her in person. The
couple quickly became "Papa John" and "Mama Jean" to us.
Their fifteen years of experience of living in our host country
had taught them valuable lessons in cross-cultural communication. Each time we were together we picked their brains,
confident that their advice would be biblically and culturally
correct. They became a set of divinely appointed parents for
us and grandparents for our children. (Later, when the Lockharts were transferred to Hong Kong, another older Canadian couple took over the parenting of our family.)

Meanwhile, as the months marched by, our own parents in
Canada were learning the art of being long-distance grandparents. "Opa" and "Oma" Klaasen gave us the best Christmas
gift imaginable: the promise of a letter each week. They were
taking seriously that grandparents should teach their grand-
children (Deut. 6). By those letters we were reminded that we
were being prayed for daily. Arriving regularly, brimming
with homey details, they eased our loneliness and made us feel
we were sharing their lives in an intimate way. Oma Klaasen
would tell us what she was cooking for supper, enclose newspaper clippings, share happenings in the lives of other family
members and tell of things that God was teaching them
through his Word, people or books.

Each letter also contained a small picture for Stephen, and
later also for Bethany. How eagerly the children now await

Oma's letters. Her thoughtful effort has paid back big dividends in our children's knowledge and appreciation of their grandparents in Canada.

We often use a cassette tape recorder. We put everything aside when a cassette arrives from family or friends. Opa and Oma include special messages, stories and songs for the children. Our children listen to these over and over, savoring the love in their grandparents' voices. We keep pictures of aunts, uncles and cousins on a bulletin board low enough for our children to see. We talk about the things we did together with these special people during our once-a-year vacations. From the time our children could hold a crayon, we encouraged them to draw special pictures for their relatives to include in our letters. Because we have been forced to put effort into building our family relationships, I think we enjoy stronger familial ties than many families who live close together.

Letters from Canada also became very important to Mark and me. They linked us with a familiar world and soothed us emotionally. Our friends acted as sounding boards for us, providing a necessary valve for all the bewildering situations in which we were finding ourselves.

An older man, a Canadian scientist, made it his special responsibility to keep us informed about the Canadian political and sports scenes. Mark, especially, looked forward to his letters telling of the triumphs of the Liberal Party or of the Toronto Maple Leafs.

An even more significant factor in minimizing our loneliness and culture shock, however, was our contact with the IVCF—Philippines. Through the IV local chapter we met Filipino believers within two weeks of our arrival in the country. David wrote in the Psalms: "I want the company of the godly men and women in the land; they are the true nobility" (Ps. 16:3). We found this to be true. Filipino believers—students and staff alike—cared for us, accepted us as we were, with all our preconceived notions and material trappings, loved us and prayed for us. They took us in, obedient to the biblical commands. They slowly and gently taught us what was acceptable in their culture and what was not. We soon discovered that in leaving our families in obedience to God, we had been brought into a much larger extended family which we had never so fully experienced before, the family of believers.

7

What Do You Do All Day?

Relatives and friends in Canada often ask, with a tinge of puzzlement and envy, "What do you do all day since you have all those maids to do the housework?" My answer to that is, "Lots! Sometimes too much." Although they respect my integrity enough to believe me, they still wonder. Imagine being suddenly released from the never-ending routines of keeping a house, but unable to hold an outside job because of visa or social restrictions imposed by the host country.

Actually, many women in such an emancipated position subconsciously resent it deeply. North American and European women tend to have their self-concept intrinsically interwoven with the management of their homes or the role they play in their chosen professions. For women subconsciously bound to being good housewives, finding that they cannot keep their homes as neat and clean in the tropics as they did in their own countries is a serious emotional blow. Being forced to hire outside help, and worse still, finding that they become dependent on that help both physically and emotionally, can be a crippling blow to their self-image. On the other hand, women who derive much of their self-respect from their professional abilities are often delighted to hand the management of their homes over to someone else. However, they may then find that their professional skills, even if needed in the local community, are not really appreciated. Such women often become vocal complainers and harbor resentment against the host country, their husband's employers or the world in general.

It is often difficult for a nonworking spouse to find meaningful work overseas. First, there is an attitude that "we always know best." One convinced that the American way is the best way is headed for uncomfortable interpersonal relationships with host country professionals. Second, to take a position that could be filled by a national professional deprives that person of employment. Third, the professional wife must either serve as a volunteer, donating all her time and skill, or work for a tiny fraction of the salary she would receive in her own country. Since in the American mind, the size of the salary and a professional's success are closely associated, volunteer-type work becomes unsavory. When volunteer work becomes unsatisfying, the volunteer often ends up taking her work less seriously, doing a halfhearted job and only working when there's nothing more exciting to do. Fourth, we love to be praised and recognized for all we do for someone else. We like to come into a host country with our particular skills and preconceived ideas and work our own revolutions. It is easy to think we have instant solutions to the problems we see. "If only the people were more efficient, if only they did things the way we do, then all their problems would be solved." Often we only create "tempests in teapots" with undisciplined, unknowledgeable efforts. But sometimes the teapot shatters, and small international incidents result.

Some people, especially after a bad experience, withdraw

from relationships with host country people and associate only with other foreigners. Bearing emotional scars and unresolved guilt, they collect the bad experiences of others to add to their tally. When they leave that country, they shake the dust off their feet. They never forget the supposed injustices they endured, recounting them again and again to other acquaintances who have had some international work experience.

For years I had fed and coddled a complaining spirit in my life. It is such a common sin among Christians that, along with worry, we don't even call it sin anymore. Instead we not only tolerate it, but we excuse or encourage it. When we have little in common with a group of people we are thrown in with by virtue of our circumstances, we soon find common ground by complaining together with them. It gives everyone something to talk about. That is an overwhelming temptation even for Christians who find themselves in cross-cultural situations. Everything is different. Everything is compared with how things were at home. The old adage that distant fields always look greener proves true. Everything in the host country's way of doing things is inefficient, unjust, dishonest, unhealthy and certainly not the best way to do it.

Christians must beware of this venomous preoccupation with complaining that they will be bombarded. It will poison their whole outlook on life if they don't resist the attack of the enemy consciously and constantly. It rapidly rots the fruit of joy, peace and patience in their lives. It erases the dividing line between truth and falsehood. It tends to fertilize seeds of bitterness.

Given these difficulties of finding a job, added to the frustrations of ignorance of the host country's language and culture, the strangeness, loneliness and an often uncomfortable climate, a Christian woman must set her mind to search for answers about what God would have her do with her time. One is tempted to let the "world around you squeeze you into its mold."

In searching for ways to work with the people in the host

country, the Christian professional has many advantages over
the non-Christian—provided she has given her own cultural
values a hard look and chosen to repent regularly of those
attitudes and values that are not Christlike. This is a continuous process. It is unnerving and uncomfortable, but tremendously rewarding and enriching in the end. The enemy,
during this process, if it is new to the believer, will often tempt
her with the feeling that she is useless and the situation is
impossible, so why try? She must be constantly alert against
becoming passive and lethargic—especially in a hot, humid
climate.

In struggling to rediscover my self-identity in my new and
bewildering situation, I found it exciting to appropriate God's
creative power. If God is Creator, then he is the source of all
true creativity. He has said in his Word that if we lack wisdom,
we are to ask and he will give it without making us feel guilty
or foolish. So I asked.

It didn't take long to get answers.

My first opportunity came as a phone call from a Dutch-
American contact who was an active, effective community
worker. She was involved in reading English storybooks to
primary schoolchildren in several local schools, as well as
building up the supply of books in their meager libraries.

Hearing that I had been trained as a teacher, she invited me
to join her. An elementary-school principal had asked her if
anyone could teach the primary teachers more about teaching
English as a second language. I protested that I was hardly
qualified to teach the teachers. She encouraged me with the
Dutch proverb that "in the land of the blind one eye is king." I
knew how little I had to offer, but there wasn't anyone else
able or willing to fill the request. I wanted to learn something
about the Filipino school system, so I accepted.

When I look back, my naiveté was astounding. I was pregnant and hardly in the country six weeks, when I started
making trips down to the large school in town several times
a week, with the mission of teaching English more effectively.
I relied heavily on my previous years of elementary teaching

for methods and materials. Since they were using mostly sight vocabulary and some phonetics to teach the children, I was able to help them by adding structural analysis to their other two techniques. I was by far the greatest beneficiary in the whole project, however. They taught me far more than I taught them.

For several years following I read two days a week to children in various classes, attempting to give the overworked classroom teachers a small break, the children some extra pleasure and maybe a few new words for their vocabulary. One great side benefit for me was that I became familiar with some of the townspeople. When I went marketing around the town, little groups of children would stop and point me out to their relatives and then shyly and formally approach me and say, "Good morning, Mrs. Klaasen." Having a tiny wedge into the local Filipino community made me relax and feel less strange.

Several months after I had started teaching, when our twin baby Andrew died, all the teachers who had been in my seminars attended the funeral and came to the graveyard. Receiving their condolences, I was overwhelmed by their concern for me as a new foreigner.

I stopped going to the schools during my difficult second pregnancy. But my interest in the needs of the schools continued. I couldn't help but notice the lack of facilities and school supplies. Every scrap of paper was recycled. Books and materials to make teaching aids were lacking. I also noticed that in our international housing area, most people had acquired the habit of generating large amounts of garbage, much of which could have been easily recycled to the public schools. There were tin cans, cardboard boxes, glass jars, paper with one side clean, used toys, scraps of cloth, all being daily tossed into forty garbage cans. But someone had to advertise the need and act as a depot and delivery person. That was something I could easily do, so I did. Friends in the United States who had lived in the Philippines and knew of the need for books kept sending boxes by sea mail. My helpers and I sorted them according to the needs of particular schools and periodically delivered them. A service that meets a real need is always welcomed. Teachers in those schools reciprocated by sending thank-you letters and inviting me to special school functions as a guest of honor.

Also, teaching Japanese women in my neighborhood conversational English on a one-to-one basis was mutually rewarding. That opportunity gave me an appreciation of Japanese art and culture I couldn't have gained in quite the same way elsewhere. At first I found the exact reciprocity of the relationships disconcerting. In traditional Japanese culture every service or small gift must be immediately reciprocated to the giver by something of similar value. I learned to accept it, however, and now find myself reciprocating naturally and enjoying this opportunity to give.

People living in North America have no comprehension of the extra amounts of time that must be spent in managing an American-style house in a tropical climate. There is about three times the cleaning and laundry. Maids are helpful but they aren't machines. Servants must be trained carefully. Sometimes they break appliances that take much time and effort to have repaired. Instructions must be given very carefully, because the language barrier is often formidable and always frustrating. I never before appreciated what Solomon wrote about the virtuous woman: "She rises . . . and plans the day's work for her servant girls" (Prov. 31:15). Teaching, training, checking on the household help you employ is a time-consuming process: I found a timetable for major cleaning jobs and a cleaning manual helpful in training and scheduling their work.

Planning, shopping and cooking for large official dinner parties becomes another standard feature in a wife's lifestyle abroad. Recipes have to be adjusted to locally available ingredients and tested beforehand to see if they are as good as they sound. The dietary restrictions of various people on the guest list must be taken into consideration when planning the menu. For example, will vegetarians be able to eat only the rice and pickles on your menu? Cooking itself is considerably more time consuming, since convenience foods may be very expensive, insect infested or completely unavailable.

If her household is running smoothly and she can find no way to employ her professional skills, a foreign wife can easily have more time on her hands than she's ever had before. She almost always has surplus money. The rent on their house may be subsidized and their salary may be tax-free combined with a lower cost of living than in their own country. Such factors can add up to a pattern of carefree spending. Since we North Americans are the last of the big spenders anyway, being able to afford handcrafted items, teak furniture, textiles and jewels from many different countries, at a fraction of the American price, results in an overwhelming temptation to make one's time abroad one long shopping spree. It's easy to rationalize, "Oh, but it's so cheap (by American standards), and besides I'll never have a chance to buy this again." In fact, in American culture, shopping has become synonymous with entertainment in many of our minds. In a foreign country, with an amazing variety of things to buy that one has never seen before, shopping becomes even more entertaining than it was at home. If a Christian gets lured into this materialistic trap, greed soon baits one further. We aren't satisfied with one string of Mikimoto pearls or one Sri Lankan batik; we want more. That this is poor stewardship of our time and resources is difficult to see when one is caught up in such a situation. Only a sense of priorities and obedience to God in stewardship can give a believer a sense of direction and peace in this aspect of life.

Early in our marriage we decided not to buy any decorative objects for our home, believing that it was an unnecessary expenditure. We already had more than enough to decorate our home adequately. We have basically held to that decision in the years abroad, thereby saving me much time, money and frustration in feeling I had to shop for curios. We certainly don't lack such things, though, because friends keep bringing them as gifts. We enjoy having them because each is a tangible evidence of our relationship with the giver. We often buy native handcrafts as gifts for others, trying as much as possible to buy from cottage industries run by believers.

Card games, especially bridge, seem to be regularly organized in most areas where foreigners live. Usually they are linked to some local charity. After a morning of cards, snacks and visiting, the women each give a donation to fund the chosen charitable organization. The charities seldom require much personal involvement from the donors, which may well be satisfactory to both donors and recipients. Since I don't enjoy card games and have many other demands on my time, I've chosen not to involve myself in this social activity in our community.

Going to and giving morning coffee parties can also take a large chunk of time. These coffees in an international community are often used to welcome newcomers and say farewell to those who are leaving. Such times can be profitable if they are well planned by the hostess; or they can be little more than times to exchange tidbits of gossip and gobs of complaints while munching calorie-laden pastries. One creative solution to making such a party more meaningful is to have various old-timers tell the group about services, activities and entertainments available in the local community. For example, someone can tell about classes to take at the university, where to buy fresh milk, which hairdresser to patronize and so forth. For a *despedida,* or farewell party, each person in the neighborhood can bring a single page for a scrapbook for the guest of honor. The accumulated book ends up being more creative and memorable than any souvenir one could buy.

My investment of a small amount of time in one particular area has yielded tremendous dividends in personal satisfaction. I encouraged a young Filipino couple to use their artistic skills to start a cottage industry. Melissa and Benito had been leaders in the local IVCF group. Soon after their marriage I noticed Mely's artistic skills in the way she kept her tiny home. She always wrote me thank-you notes for the little gifts I brought her as *pasalubong.* I noted that each card was a work of art. Line, scale, color, balance and rhythm were attractively combined in each card. At Christmastime, I gave her the basic idea and materials to make several hundred cards for us to send to friends and colleagues (according to the Asian custom as well as the American one). The result was a delight. The Christian message was enhanced by the art decorating each card. Mely started making note paper, invitations and thank-you cards for me. Almost invariably the recipients would comment on the beauty of those handmade cards. Since Ben was still a student, and their three babies arrived in rapid succession, the extra income from making the cards was necessary for their economic survival. Before long I saw how to increase their sales by having them make cards for me to sell to my neighbors. Later, Little Red Riding Hood dolls and Quiet Books were added to their cottage industry.

In the early years I was their principal salesperson, selling their products to my neighbors in the international community. Many were delighted to buy such careful craftsmanship and, by the purchase, help this couple as well. Today Ben and Mely employ several women and out-of-school youth, all new believers, after having painstakingly taught them the skills. As the women work in her crowded living room several days each week, sewing and embroidering, Mely listens to their problems and counsels them as an older sister in Christ. It is beautiful to see how this growing cottage industry provides for the bodies and the souls of the people involved in it. The wholeness of the good news exemplified in the lives of these people is as attractive as the products their hands produce.

I wish I had spent more time in my early years in the Philippines learning the national language, and reading more of the history and literature of the country. Learning any language takes hard, disciplined work. There is no other way to do it. In our position, almost all the host-country people we associate with are professionals with an excellent grasp of English, so we've been lazy in applying ourselves to learn the national language. Since one must be self-motivated to find a tutor and to practice, it's easy to take the route of least effort and not even try. It's basically an ego-problem again. We're embarrassed to use a language if we can't do it perfectly. We're afraid of being laughed at. We always want to be the best, the teacher. In learning a language one must be willing to start at the very bottom, as a pupil who may even appear stupid.

Reading the history and literature of the host country also takes discipline. It is a necessity, however, for a Christian who wants to become more knowledgeable about, and more understanding of, the local situation. It is a believer's responsibility to make the effort. With a little knowledge, one can spare oneself many blunders and much grief. One must also be able to look at history from both sides of the page, theirs and yours. The two often conflict. The believer must be willing to say, "We were wrong there . . . and there . . . and there. . . . I'm sorry."

One evening during an international conference I found myself seated next to the Indonesian minister of agriculture at dinner. He picked up my place card and read my name. As he neatly replaced the card, I immediately read his mind in the tone of his voice, "Ah, Mrs. Klaasen. Are you Dutch?" (I remember what your people did to us!)

"No . . . and yes," I stammered, "but I'm sorry for what my ancestors did wrongly to your people," I added meekly.

With that barely whispered admission out of my mouth, his attitude toward me changed and softened. He spent most of the next hour telling me about some of the deep problems he faced in his office. The problems always came back to having their roots in the sinfulness of human nature. It was one of the most meaningful conversations I've ever had with a politician. There was a redemptive quality to it that wouldn't have been possible if the Holy Spirit hadn't nudged me during our introductions.

For Christians, learning how to use the time and opportunities God gives us is never a static situation, but a progressive experience. In North American culture we look on time almost as a god, who either sits still, leering and hanging heavy on our hands, or flies by, stealing our desires of things we wanted to do with him. In spite of that we often worship him.

The biblical view of time is different. All of it is God's gift. We look at time in history and know there will be a culmination, an end, when Jesus Christ will return. That glorious fact influences how we decide to use the time we have been given. We pray with the psalmist: "Teach us to number our days and recognize how few they are; help us to spend them as we should" (Ps. 90:12).

8

Join the Local Church

A neighbor of ours, now living in her third host country, remarked even before she was a convinced Christian: "The best place to get to know the people of the country is through the local church. In service organizations and bridge parties—even in the charities—you don't have much chance to really know the people."

For Mark and me there was not much temptation to stay away from the Filipino church in our community. The Scriptures were clear. We were not to neglect assembling together with believers. The church was the only place we thought we could find them.

At that time, as Protestants, we had the choice of an established United Church of Christ congregation with a national pastor, or a Baptist mission led by American missionaries. The choice was difficult because the Baptist theology was closer to

ours than that of the UCCP. But the Baptist mission was
located five miles from our home and the UCCP chapel was
only a half mile away. We decided it would be wiser to attend
a community church whose members we were likely to en-
counter during the week. There was also the language barrier: the Baptist mission used Filipino whereas the chapel
used English. Later on, our decision was severely tested when
some members of our congregation disagreed with us on
biblical authority in matters of faith and practice. Yet we never
felt led to leave that congregation when the going got rough.

We were almost immediately given all kinds of opportunities to serve in the program of that old established church.
The congregation was made up almost totally of professional
people or students connected with the university campus
across the street from the chapel.

There was no Sunday-school class for college students, so
when my husband was asked to start one, he did. There was
no Sunday morning adult discussion group, so several others
and I became the core of such a weekly group. We needed
Sunday-school materials. Knowing Papa John, still involved
in publishing Christian materials, made it easier for me to
get them.

As years went by and the local people came to know us better, they felt freer to ask us for help.

The Scriptures had been a relatively closed book for that
congregation. The pastors of the denomination seemed to be
in a phase of preaching a fashionable type of liberation theology that was largely political in orientation. Ferment and
rebellion, coupled with student strikes and demonstrations,
were popular in our community during those years. Church-
goers were not taught to look to biblical authority for guidelines for the unsettling daily situations.

Mark and I searched for the meaning of Micah 6:8 in our
lives: "He has told you what he wants, and this is all it is: to
be fair and just and merciful, and to walk humbly with your
God." How were we to teach that command to those we were
teaching in the church?

We had to learn new ways to practice what we preached, starting with the way we treated our own employees, in our home and in the office. Salaries had to be more than fair; there had to be concern for the welfare of the whole person. With the non-Christian American attitude of "Mind your own business; don't get involved," such concern wasn't easy to put into practice. "To be just and merciful" were costly commands, we discovered.

Mark didn't endear himself to his employees by consistently checking up on the accuracy of submitted expense accounts. His desire for honesty and fairness in dealings with both employees and employer often left him in the midst of a crossfire. Misunderstandings and slanderings were part of the price to be paid for doing justice.

Since there were no secrets in the community the church members soon heard such stories. "To walk humbly with our God" was even more difficult. Auntie Mary, an elderly, vivacious Chinese saint, explained that in Chinese characters that phrase meant "going God's way instead of your own way." Learning to obey that command seems to be a continuous process.

We were so overeager to change the church. We wanted to see changes in the life and practice of the congregation, making them like some perfect, imaginary congregation—which will probably be found only in heaven. How our pastors suffered under our constant suggestions and lack of personal acceptance! Our resentment and judgmental attitudes against the content of their sermons *bound* them, making it difficult for the Holy Spirit to do the work in them he was longing to do.

What is the church? What should it be?

As a new believer and a young university student, ensconced for the first time in a caring, vibrant Bible study group, I had become self-righteously indignant about the denominational church. It was sterile. Ineffective. Class-concious. Cold. Self-seeking. It certainly didn't care much about university students. (Especially the loud-mouthed kind.) I didn't need to bother about that kind of church. I could shake the dust off my feet and walk right back into the arms of the warm, responsive IVCF group on campus. There people understood me. They prayed about my problems. Our prayers got specific answers. And so the Christian student organization became my "church," while the denominational church was a place to which I went for a couple of hours each Sunday in order to do my duty and put up a good appearance. (I wasn't an honest rebel.)

Later, during graduate school days, we found churches with good expository teaching where we felt a responsibility to pitch in by teaching in the Sunday school and helping with music. But our real church was still the small IVCF Bible study group on campus. The unrepented seed-sins of our critical attitudes toward the standard denominational church remained in us. We had never learned to see certain attitudes as sin: a critical spirit, hardness, unbelief ("They'll never change no matter what we do"), self-righteousness and constant judgment of what was wrong with both the members and the institution. I read articles on the decline of the organized church with unholy zeal. Such writings supported my hypothesis: the organized church was a sitting duck, soon to be dead for sure.

Many Christian students who have tuned into Jesus Christ during their college years tune out after graduation. They say they are disillusioned by the organized church. They repeat a lengthy list of its sins, but as we did, they forget to repent of their own. They forget the command of the Lord Jesus to disciple wherever they are, whomever they meet.

Anne Ortlund's book *Up with Worship* deals with this problem. Basically she says that if you're a member of a dead church, repent of your stultifying sin-filled attitudes toward it, get together with one or two like-minded believers, pray and pray and pray, and then work as if everything depends on you. But above all, keep repenting of your own critical attitudes. Be tenderhearted, forgiving one another as Christ Jesus has forgiven you.

Unhappily for both us and the Filipino church, it took us five years to learn that our very own sin had held back the growth that we thought we so desperately wanted to see in that church. For the first time since we were university students, for a period of time we didn't have the warmth and comfort of a small Bible study group. The denominational church was all we had.

Over those years there were plenty of opportunities to speak, lead Bible studies, give, help and advise as members of the church council. Somehow all that service wasn't satisfying. Worse still, it didn't appear to bring any results. We were often disappointed and resentful about the lack of life in our church. Then we got tired. We seemed to be trying to fill a bottomless pail with water. Someone has said that discouragement is the Enemy's most effective weapon. So much of our physical and emotional energy was going into helping keep the church afloat that I grew increasingly bitter. The situation wasn't helped by the fact that at the Baptist Church, now under national leadership, aggressive evangelism and sound Bible teaching were affecting increasing numbers of people. Their congregation was growing so rapidly that they were overflowing their facilities.

I came very close to an emotional collapse. But God is faithful and kind. He made my husband sensitive to my spiritual need, even though Mark couldn't exactly pinpoint the root problem. As a birthday gift that spring, he had ordered a copy of Catherine Marshall's newly published *Something More*.

That Easter, in desperate need, I lay in bed and read. There was no joy in going to the Easter Sunrise Service. After all, our church had chosen to cooperate with the Catholics on that instead of with the Baptists. There was no joy in the fact of the resurrection that year. No power. No energy. Every job around the house became an impossible mountain to move. Even reading to our children for a few minutes became an exhausting imposition. My maids, puzzled by my strange sickness, tiptoed about as they managed the house. They felt the gloom and depression that poisoned the atmosphere.

I was in such a state because my subconscious mind was stacked so full of unforgiveness and resentment against people who had touched my life from years before until the present. All my psychic energy was being used to keep those skeletons in the closet. I didn't want to remember them. They stank. They hurt too much to be remembered. My accumulating resentments against our church were merely the last straw in a long process. But at that time I didn't know the nature of my problem.

So I lay on my rumpled bed, shades drawn in my air-conditioned room, and doggedly read. When I finished chapter three, "Forgiveness: The Aughts and the Anys," I could go no further. Up until then I had given mere intellectual assent to the spiritual concepts of the preceding two chapters. Now the hand of truth was a choking one. Either I learned to forgive, or I died. It was as starkly simple as that.

But the battle to choose the way of forgiveness wasn't simple. St. Paul wrote that we don't wrestle against people but against principalities and powers. That Easter Sunday I had an initiation into that kind of battle. The big *I*, which wanted to reserve many rights for itself (including the right to pass judgment on every person and situation that touched my life), wasn't about to lie down and die.

A fragment of realization pierced my battle-weary mind. It was I, myself, who had to strike the deathblow to my own ego. With that the tide of battle turned. Jesus is always victorious. Feebly I dragged my unwilling will to his side. Respite came. Then I finally saw that forgiveness is a decision of the will. It is not a feeling. I had to decide to will to forgive a person of a particular wrong. The act of forgiveness didn't depend on whether that person had been right or wrong in the particular incident. He or she could be wrong as wrong could be. My business was to forgive, not to judge.

I copied the short prayer that Catherine Marshall had suggested onto a small card and later tacked it to the bulletin board above my desk. It went something like this:

Lord, I release _____ from my judgment. Forgive

me that I may have bound him and hampered your work by judging him. Now I step out of the way so that heaven can go into action for _____. Thank you, Holy Spirit, that you are already at work in _____.

For several weeks as I sat at my desk, my work was often interrupted. Someone had to be "released." Scores of people had to be released, going back to my early childhood. People who had said true or false things about me or my family. Relatives, neighbors, public figures, former teaching colleagues, people at our local church, our pastors. The process seemed to be endless, but it was not burdensome. With each release, a fresh load of emotional debris was cleared out of my subconscious mind. When the cross of Jesus covered those past hurts and resentments, they were struck out, powerless to hurt and chain me any longer.

The results of that massive housecleaning were many. A lightness, an indescribable buoyancy, permeated my mind. The ordinary activities of the day were no longer burdensome, people no longer had to be endured. I didn't have to steel myself and by sheer willpower do the good works that I thought the Word of God demanded of me.

Fear and anxiety had been my two constant companions through all our years abroad. I had repented of them daily, sometimes many times. My journal contained an almost daily entry which read: "Lord Jesus, I feel so worried and anxious about _____. Please forgive me. Thank you that you have." But no matter how often I repeated that prayer, meaning it to the best of my ability, fear and anxiety dogged me. I was afraid of the vendors in the market, certain that each one was out to cheat me. I was afraid of being robbed. Afraid of being misunderstood. Afraid of appearing uncultured and unsophisticated to my neighbors. Afraid I couldn't cook well enough. Afraid my maids weren't trained well enough compared with those of my neighbors. Now, suddenly, I realized that I was repenting of fear and anxiety much less than previously. Those twin sins didn't hound me anymore. I was free.

Much later I discovered the psychological reason behind

that spiritual victory. In *Prayer Can Change Your Life,* William R. Parker and Elaine St. John wrote that "ninety per cent of our fears are rooted in resentment." As I was forgiving people and releasing them from my judgment, resentment was being cleared out at the same time, and with it the fertile ground that had nurtured fear.

For several months afterward, I would dream vividly of other people who had hurt me, or whom I had hurt. After the dream I would wake up, my mind instantly alert. Then after I prayed the Prayer of Release, forgiving them, deep peaceful sleep came almost immediately. The beam of the night watchman's flashlight moving across our tiled ceiling no longer jolted me awake. I had resented the guard's audacity to shine his light into our bedroom, but now, instead, I felt thankful for the security he represented. I would snuggle into my cool pillow, content and grateful.

In the process of loosing all those people that I had blindly bound by my putrefying self-righteousness, I discovered that I had bound myself along with them. Now love began to flow. I didn't have to wear myself out any longer trying to generate interest in other people. When I was clean before God, that interest came easily, naturally. Hope seemed renewed, even without tangible evidence that the Holy Spirit was doing anything new.

That August my faith and hope were much increased when our church decided to have an evangelism emphasis month. It was a new concept for our congregation. How should we begin? Whom should we get to help us?

Years before, I had seen a panel truck with a neatly lettered sign, "Lay Witness Mission—Philippines (Methodist)" on one of Manila's busy thoroughfares. I had immediately associated that organization with Faith at Work in Canada. It would be interesting to know more about this Philippine-based group, I had mused, but merely filed the information away mentally for future reference.

While brainstorming in the evangelism committee meeting, I remembered that group. How could we get in touch with them? Perhaps the president of the Methodist Deaconess' School in Manila would know of them. I was appointed by the committee to search for the group to see if they would lead a weekend retreat in our church.

The president of the ladies' college was cordially helpful. The leader of the group was out of the country, but the man presently in charge worked at the Central Bank. She could telephone a friend who probably had his number. Contact was established.

Yes, they'd love to come. In fact, they wanted to come for a planning and training day two weeks before the actual retreat. That was fine with us. We were impressed that they would invest so much time and effort in us.

When the day of the training meeting arrived, a dozen people showed up from Manila, but only a scant half-dozen from our own congregation. But our guests appeared unruffled by the meager attendance and lack of enthusiasm.

Consumed with curiosity, I looked them over carefully. Introductions revealed that they represented a wide range professionally: mining executive, dean of nursing, feed store owner, Bible teacher, bank supervisor. They certainly looked as if they would fit in with our congregation, these middle-class Methodists. I heaved a sigh of relief. If they didn't, oh dear! Who had suggested that we get them in the first place?

Then they started to sing. The accordionist pulled out all the stops. Their voices soared with enthusiasm and conviction. "I love the Lord with all my heart, all my soul, all my strength. With all that is within me, Praise his holy name." Scripture-based songs poured out. Their hands clapped and feet tapped to the rhythm of the music. "Oh no," I thought, "they're really pentecostals! Whatever will we do?"

The Bible teacher got up and expounded a single verse: "If my people will humble themselves and pray, and search for me, and turn from their wicked ways, I will hear them from heaven and forgive their sins and heal their land" (2 Chron. 7:14). Systematically, enthusiastically, she taught us the meaning of each phrase of that command and promise.

There was undeniable power in her message. God, the Holy Spirit, was speaking.

There it was again. I was to humble myself. That meant going God's way, and not my own. Still, the team was more emotional than I liked groups to be. I prided myself on my sound, rational approach when it came to all matters of faith and practice. I didn't want to let go of my preconceived ideas of what would appeal to our highly intellectual congregation.

That afternoon the bank supervisor explained the procedures for the small groups. The materials they had were biblically based. They carefully explained the interrelations of God to people and people to people.

At the end of the afternoon our visitors taught us to sing a song based on Matthew 6:33—" 'Seek ye first the kingdom of God, and his righteousness; and all these things shall be added unto you.' Alleluia. Alleluia."

That was my problem. I wasn't seeking God's righteousness, but my own.

Near dusk we waved goodbye to the Lay Witness team. Our pastor and I looked at each other but didn't say anything for a while. That didn't matter. We read each other's thoughts: "Wow. What are we in for? How will they go over with our congregation?"

In our minds fear mingled with hope, confusion with purpose. We both went home to pray and work. Our pastor visited every family in the congregation in the next two weeks, personally encouraging them to attend the retreat.

The Saturday of the retreat dawned cloudless and bright after a week of typhoon squalls. "Someone's even been praying about the weather," I thought, knowing that drizzly weather would drastically cut attendance.

The Lay Witness team and their associates arrived at our church earlier than most of the local people. They were well organized. Folding chairs were set up in groups of ten under the spreading mango trees in the churchyard. Everyone received a color-coded name tag, the color denoting the small group we would be in later that morning.

The song leader and accordionist took their places and immediately started to teach Scripture songs to the group as they continued to assemble. We joined in, hesitantly at first. The beat of their music shocked us somewhat; we were more used to Bach and Mendelssohn.

Because ours was an international congregation, the team had thought it appropriate to invite an American missionary as guest speaker for two special sermons during the weekend. Though a soft-spoken man in private, behind the pulpit his voice thundered as he challenged us to think through the priorities in our lives. Whom were we going to serve, God or ourselves? Although I could agree with his message, its style of delivery left me decidedly uncomfortable. Finally, that was over. Time to go to the small groups.

There were people in our group whom I was surprised to see, people I hadn't expected to take off a Saturday for such a retreat. One was Linda, a professor's wife. A former beauty queen, for years she had gone from one state of emotional exhaustion to another, and consequently had been the brunt of much congregational and community gossip. She had an attentive husband, four intelligent children, an adequate home, a large wardrobe. Why couldn't she pull herself together? Why did she feel so sorry for herself? So wagged all the knowing tongues.

In January the Holy Spirit had nudged me to visit this woman, but I had been unwilling to obey. I had no obvious reason to go. She rarely came to church. I hardly knew her. So I made excuse after excuse during the next few months whenever the conviction to visit her came. I didn't go. Now she was sitting beside me at this retreat, in the same small group.

After introductions, the guest leader in our group said that now was the time for us to open our hearts, our lives, to one another. She shared several recent experiences of God's love and care for her as a widow with small children and as a professional social worker. There was a genuineness, a validity to her story that captivated us. When she finished she encouraged us to share what was on our hearts. Several people mentioned that they hadn't wanted to come to the retreat, but were now glad to be here.

During their testimonies Linda was clearly agitated. The leader noticed her discomfort, too, and gently encouraged her to share her story. It was as though a floodgate had been sprung. She started to pour out the miseries and injustices she had endured over the years, compounded by loneliness and a sense of alienation and lack of acceptance from members of the various churches she had attended. Linda wanted to help the church, she wanted to be a good Protestant, but her help was never appreciated or reciprocated. I listened, stunned by each new sordid revelation. I remembered uncomfortably how often I had refused to make the effort to visit her when the idea had crossed my mind. When she finished, I had to confess to the group my sin of neglect against her and disobedience toward God. The group pulled their chairs closer together and prayed for both of us.

After lunch, Linda asked me if I could drive her two daughters to their ballet lessons in order to save time so that she wouldn't have to take public transportation and miss much of the afternoon session. I gladly complied. As we slid onto the searing vinyl seat of our station wagon, she asked, "Do you think you could come up to my house two or three times a week to study the Bible with me? The Jehovah's Witnesses used to come two times a week for several years. I almost joined them. In fact I was going to be baptized, but when the day came, I got very sick and couldn't go. So in the end I never joined them."

I hesitated. "Well, I guess we might be able to work something out. Maybe once a week?" My mind went through a series of gymnastics. With my present timetable, how could I fit in one more regular thing each week? I didn't know. Yet she was so pathetically eager.

Linda seemed partially pacified with the promise of a once-a-week meeting. We returned to the church after the children had been delivered to their various destinations.

It was a hot, lazy afternoon. Hardly a breeze wafted through the open shutters. Some people had gone home to nap in cooler, more comfortable places. Others sat on the hard pews with glazed looks in their eyes; the fried chicken lunch had been filling indeed. The songleader and accordionist, however, didn't lack enthusiasm. They had us sing and sing and sing. The lethargy lifted and finally most of us were awake. The final item on the afternoon program was sharing time, a time for people to tell each other what they had learned that day. Linda grasped the opportunity to make a clean break with her past, with all its injustices and hurts. For forty minutes she clutched the podium and wrenched out ugly memories, displaying them with abandonment to the group. Torrents of tears added cleansing to her emotional and spiritual housecleaning. We who sat and listened didn't know how to react. Would she be so ashamed of her public performance that she would never face any of us again? Would she really know, experientially, that Jesus had forgiven her? Or was she just going crazy before our very eyes? Finally, the leader led her gently from the podium and publicly prayed for her that she would know the healing that the Holy Spirit was offering her immediately. The rest of us prayed too, for her—and for ourselves.

At the close of the afternoon the dozen or so people on the Lay Witness Mission team stood in a semicircle in the chancel and sang again, "Seek ye first the kingdom of God and his righteousness." The slanting rays of the afternoon sun told us that time had been forgotten that afternoon.

The team squeezed our hands, said goodbye until tomorrow and declared repeatedly that they would pray for us. The jeep drivers revved up their engines, the team and their associates squeezed in. As they turned out of the churchyard we could see their waving hands and radiant faces above a cloud of dust.

It had been an emotionally draining afternoon. We were left with an ambivalent feeling. What would tomorrow morning be like? More of the congregation would be there on a Sunday morning. How would they respond to the loud-voiced American who was to preach the sermon? It had been whispered about that he really only got warmed up after the first hour of preaching. Some things about today had been good, some so-so. But what about tomorrow? We just didn't know.

Sunday morning began busy. I was scheduled to help administer several new Sunday-school classes that we were starting that day. There was hardly time to think about what would happen during the regular worship service. The Lay Witness team had arrived from Manila early, hopeful and expectant of the good things the Holy Spirit was going to do that day. I barely had time to direct them to the adult Sunday-school class before flying off to my other responsibilities. Somehow the bright assurance evidenced in their personalities calmed my wondering heart.

With my extra Sunday-school work that morning I was almost late for the worship service and barely got a seat. The grapevine had certainly worked more effectively than the telephone. The church was packed. Obviously the people who had heard our guest preacher the day before had been more favorably impressed with his message and method of delivery than I had been. They had told all their friends to come.

Our service started out as orderly as usual. Then several special duets were sung in close harmony in the Full Gospel style by the speaker's wife and daughter. The style made me uncomfortable. After what seemed like an eternity, it was time for the guest preacher. It didn't take him long to get warmed up. The man in charge of the PA system soon slipped out to turn it down. Our guest certainly didn't need any help from the loud-speaker. I sat riveted to my seat and prayed, oblivious to the message. This wasn't at all what these people were used to hearing in sermon or service. What if they started to get up and walk out en masse? But no one did. In front of me three high-schoolers were quietly heckling the speaker. As the sermon went on, however, and got louder and louder, the fellows in front of me became quieter and quieter. I desperately prayed on, fighting trepidation as the minutes inched toward noon.

The preacher reached a final crescendo and made a call to commitment to the congregation. To my amazement, so many people went forward to the chancel signifying that they wanted to follow Jesus Christ that there was hardly room for them all at the front of the church. Tears overwhelmed me, as I sat and repented of my unbelief. God, the Holy Spirit, wasn't limited in the ways he chose to speak to people's minds and hearts, bringing them back to himself. Through my streaming tears, I saw Filipinos and foreigners, professors and students, grandmothers and children standing before us. The high-school hecklers were there too.

"Thank you, Jesus. Thank you" was all I could whisper.

Later, while the bright tropical sun dried our tear-stained faces, we stood with our pastor in the churchyard, amazed, and we rejoiced together.

"I don't know when this has happened in our church before," he said. "Did you see _____? and _____? and _____? Even my own daughter!" He shook his head in wonder and praised God. We joined him joyfully.

Somehow in the early morning rush I had obeyed the nudge of the Spirit to put a large pork roast in the oven, dousing it with thyme, ginger and soy sauce before leaving for Sunday school. I had instructed one of our helpers to prepare pilaf from five cups of raw rice. "I don't know whether we'll have six or sixteen guests for lunch," I warned.

The roast would be ready by now, so it was easy to extend hospitality to the Lay Witness team and our pastor and some of the elders.

What a celebration that Sunday lunch hour was! We were walking on air, hardly knowing whether we had dreamed or actually experienced what the Holy Spirit had started in our church in the past few hours. The Lay Witness team was more poised and assured. They, having more faith than we, had expected him to work, and of course he had. When it was time to say goodbye, the dozen and a half of us made a huge semicircle around the piano and raised our voices as a choir. "I love the Lord with all my heart, and soul and mind. and strength. With all that is within me, Praise his holy name." I looked from one radiant face to another, Methodist pentecostals, Full Gospel preacher, staid former Presbyterians and two Mennonites. I glimpsed a bit of heaven as I looked.

There were those who weren't revived, who were critical of that massive show of emotion one August Sunday morning. There are others who still come and go, searching for what or for whom they aren't quite certain. There are eager inquirers who want to study the Word of God, but there aren't enough lay teacher-pastors to help them. The pastor is overworked and underpaid according to some members, and the reverse according to others.

I didn't really want to take the time to disciple Linda, but she maneuvered me into a position where I couldn't refuse. Late every Wednesday afternoon, most often weary and sticky-hot from the day's activities, I would pick up my toddler, Bethany, and leave instructions for a simple supper with our helpers. Then I picked up another Christian sister, Lumen, and her daughter and slowly drove the miles up the mountain to Linda's bungalow. As I parked the car beside her garden, creatively landscaped with dozens of different ornamental plants and flowers, interspersed with fruit trees, she would emerge from the house, two daughters in tow to welcome ours.

"Welcome, welcome," she would call, "I'm so glad you came."

The next hour would fly by as she drank in every promise of the Word of God for her life. Eagerly she would report on how application of the past week's Bible study had worked in her life. She took the warnings and commands of the Word utterly seriously. Her enthusiasm was contagious, exciting in me the wonder of old truths reborn in Linda's life. Later, Lumen and I switched places; she became the leader and I the co-leader. Linda invited friends who were interested in studying the Word to join us. They came, often more curious about the obvious change in her life than about the Bible per se.

Every Wednesday night I was late for supper. But it didn't matter. I came home refreshed and gladdened because of Linda. The Holy Spirit was teaching me so much through her life. She is one of many precious gifts that have come our way because we joined the local church.

9

No Survival without the Body of Christ

For years the term "body of Christ" was somewhat of an enigma to me. If someone had asked for a definition, I would have said that it's the real church, the groups of true believers, contrasted with the church as a building or a denomination with all its members. That's all. I suspected that scattered "true believers" could be found in every denominational church as well as outside of it. In heaven we would finally see who made up the real church, the body of Christ, when Jesus came to claim her as his bride. Other than entertaining a distant hope of seeing the body and being a part of it then, I had no knowledge or appreciation of what the body was to be here and now, or my responsibilities to it and its responsibilities to me.

After putting my commitment to God as the first priority in my life, a growing awareness of my need for contact with other believers had emerged. I longed to be with them. I wished there were Christians who could counsel us in the awkward new situations in which we found ourselves. There was joy in finding the truths of Scripture powerful and operative in my new situation, but I needed others with whom to share my joy. My sense of loneliness was assuaged from time to time by visits to Christian friends in Manila. But we lived in different social and geographical worlds. What were we to do? There seemed to be no answers other than to continue those sporadic times of fellowship—and comfort one another that in heaven we wouldn't be separated by time and place.

Before leaving Canada I had read *Sky Waves,* a history of Far East Broadcasting Company and its ministry in Asia through Christian radio programs. Consequently, on arrival in the Philippines, we tuned our radio to FEBC-Manila. One Sunday morning when we came home from early church and flipped on the radio, we heard a taped worship service from Lake Avenue Congregational Church in Pasadena, California. We were attracted by the intensity of the prayers, the quality of the music and the scholarship and warmth in the pastor's message. The next Sunday we made it a point to listen, until Sunday after Sunday that broadcast became a joyfully anticipated event of our Day of Rest. A sense of worship and adoration permeated the hour. Men and women focused away from themselves and on their Redeemer-King. Raymond Ortlund, the teaching pastor on the ministerial team, expounded the Word of God to us, applying it to everyday situations that we could readily adapt to our own lives. He seemed to do his homework well, but led his congregation from a position of weakness rather than strength. No expert or supersaint, he was like one beggar who had found food and wanted all the rest of us beggars to find the Bread of Life as well.

As the years went by, Pastor Ray taught us that each believer's life needed three broad priorities in order to have the rich wholeness God intended for his children. Those priorities were: First, commitment to God and Christ; Second, commitment to the body of Christ; Third, commitment to the work of Christ in the world. The priorities have to be applied in the order given, and all three are necessary. Commitment number one alone in the life of believers tends to produce Pharisees. An intellectual grasp of God's Word without obedience to it stagnates in our lives and breeds gross spiritual pride. On the other hand, believers who focus on the body of Christ, concentrating only on a relationship with other Christians, become parasites. Like leeches, such believers depend on others to nourish them spiritually and emotionally—and, in extreme cases, even physically. Groups often tolerate such behavior out of a sense of false guilt. Worrying that the baby Christian might die if not fed and coddled, they don't allow them to grow up. Finally, to overemphasize the third priority produces Do Gooders for whom their work in the world sooner or later becomes a humanistic ego trip. The work of doing good becomes more important than the Lord who ordained it.

Mark and I came to see that in our own lives we were trying to effect priorities one and three. Number two, however, our commitment to the body of Christ, other believers, was mostly a blank. But where were we to find them? How were we to exercise commitment to a group of people we didn't even know existed? At that time we didn't think our local church could provide such people. The truth was it could, and did, later.

As we grappled with our need for brothers and sisters, we longingly recalled the quality of love demonstrated in the IVCF group during one of our years at Macdonald College. At the beginning it had taken much emotional energy just to keep that tiny, struggling group cohesive enough to call weekly meetings. A decade ago it was tough being labeled "English" and "Protestant" in French Canada. But a dozen of us managed to meet together in the high-ceilinged ornate Stewart Room to sing, pray and hear a speaker. Mark and I were graduate students trying to encourage the undergraduate student witness. We attended the meetings regularly and "encouraged" the students by pointing out all the things they could have done better. I kept telling them of the

wonderful IVCF group back at our university in Saskatchewan, with hundreds of students attending meetings and a
score of weekly Bible study groups. The more I extolled the
wonders of our former IV group, the more lethargic and discouraged our handful of students became. It looked hopeless.
If only they would take our suggestions and put them to work.

The next fall, about a dozen new students, all transfers
from another college, joined our group. They were all matur-
ing believers and upper division students. Several more Christian foreign students newly arrived in Canada came as well.
The newcomers seemed determined to give God first priority
in their lives. The work of Christ on our campus began to take
off despite the discouraged leadership and its thorn-in-the-
flesh advisers, us.

That year twenty students from our campus went to the
IVCF Urbana Student Missionary Convention chaperoned by
a somewhat fearful Mark, worried whether the convention
scholarships had been given to the right students. The miracle
of Urbana is that non-Christians become Christians and non-
descript Christians become vigorous disciples. It happened to
the contingent from our small agricultural college. With their
eyes opened to their responsibilities for non-Christian students, they started to evangelize their classmates aggressively,
picking the ripe grapes in the Lord's vineyard.

In our IV group's elections that spring, each leadership
position was filled by a mature Christian student with definite
leadership abilities. Best of all was a serious yet joyous sense of
commitment evident not only in the newly elected council but
also among many members of the group. More than that,
several members on the IV exec carried dual responsibilities
as dons in the dorms or as members of the college student
council. The Christians were no longer a cowering timid
minority. They were out front, willing to stand up and be
counted. Like birth pangs, the discouragements of the previous year became a long-forgotten memory. Instead, like
new mothers, we anticipated the growth of our group with
much joy.

The job of Bible study leadership-coordinator had been assigned to Mark. Each Monday that autumn he spent the greater part of the day planning the week's study in a long series for the students on the book of Acts. Monday evening Mark led a Bible study composed of those who would later that week lead studies in their dorms. Mark got great satisfaction out of helping them discover the meat of the Word for themselves through inductive Bible study methods. He was passing on what he himself had been taught by older Christian students, and his willing group of leaders was passing it on to others. At each meeting they shared joys and disappointments about their individual groups and learned to pray for one another. They started building a community, helping one another, carrying one another's burdens, simply because, like the early church, they wanted to love each other. The format of the general weekly meetings didn't change much, but the atmosphere in them did. Believers wanted to get involved in one another's lives because they saw they had responsibilities to one another. The responsibilities weren't burdensome; they were shouldered with a sense of glad obedience. Prayers were answered in quiet as well as dramatic ways.

The yeast began to ferment. Theological emphasis on denominational differences within the group began to fade. When a Roman Catholic decided to give his life to Jesus, the Baptists didn't hound him to denounce his church as they might previously have done. Instead, they simply accepted him as a new brother and taught him how to have a quiet time, to get something out of that very new book, the Bible, which he may never have opened before.

Soon the editor of the campus newspaper found a new angle, publishing crude things about the local Christian group and their president, who was also the student body treasurer. The result of that adverse publicity (really a form of persecution) was positive for us. It brought many curiosity seekers to see if we were really the queer ducks and pious prudes we were made out to be in the campus "rag." In the end, it wasn't so much the message that impressed those inquirers, but the love within our group. Here was a group of Christians, a body of believers, who were learning to love each other. What a compelling attractive force love is! It became the most powerful factor for evangelism. Out of this love, spiritual babies started to be born with remarkable regularity.

It could have been a long dreary winter, since much of my physical energy that winter was sapped by my demanding teaching job and the recurring infection. But it wasn't. Those students showered their love on me. They came to sit on my bed and share with me the excitement of what they were learning in the Word of God, the answers to prayer. They came to cook delectable Chinese dishes in our kitchen. They mopped, dusted, scoured the bathtub and folded the laundry.

I remember Ani, daughter of a wealthy Armenian shirt manufacturer, peering into my face anxiously as I dragged myself up the long flight of stairs after school late one Friday afternoon, calling, "Are you all right? Sheila couldn't come today to clean the apartment because she has a term paper overdue. She said you really needed help, so I said I'd come. Would you come and look at the way I cleaned the stove and see if it's all right before you go to bed?"

"Why, of course, it's all right, Ani!" I replied. I wanted only to head straight for my bed. I was numbly grateful that someone else was willing to take over some of the never-ending cleaning chores.

She insisted, "Please come and check."

I followed her into the long narrow kitchen and looked at the gleaming stove surface, assuring her that the job met a home ec teacher's standards.

"Oh, I'm so glad it's OK!" she said with a happy sigh of relief. "I spent three hours on it. It's the first time in my life I've cleaned a stove and I didn't know quite how to do it."

I looked at her again. She was a picture out of a Breck shampoo ad, her hair perfectly shaped by a Sassoon stylist. The sleeves of her French lemon-yellow wool sweater were pulled up over her elbows. Then I looked at her hands, small, tapering fingers with the nail polish now chipped, cuticles encrusted with grime and skin pale and wrinkled from the hot water and scouring powder. Ani, used to being waited on but newly born into the family of God, had freely and lovingly served me in my need. That was just one of the tangible evidences of the love from our growing body of Christ.

That year ended with a triumphant banquet, many hours long, as student after student rose to tell what the fellowship had meant to them that year. About two hundred people attended the dinner, among them university faculty, Protestant pastors and Roman Catholic priests, attracted not only by the campus ferment but by the glow of the Spirit.

All the key leaders seemed to graduate that year. Next year's group was much smaller again and perhaps a bit cowed by the glories of the previous year.

The demands of finishing Mark's thesis seemed to justify our staying out of undergraduate student activities that year. Instead, a small group of graduate students, mostly from foreign countries, met in our apartment on Sunday evenings for Bible study and prayer. Our group had problems with language barriers and with differences in spiritual maturity. Some, separated from their families, were intensely lonely. Others carried scars of emotional disturbances from family problems. We were a mixed bag. But we hung in together and the Holy Spirit taught us through his Word and through one another. They prayed Mark's thesis through to completion, encouraging him to finish it before leaving the campus. Often he would gladly have thrown it into a box and said, "I'll get on to my job and finish the thing after I'm working." That would have been jumping from the frying pan into the fire, as many graduate students who have tried it will testify.

Having had such good fellowship in Canada, our desire grew for the same in the Philippines. But that took several years. We missed having a group of believers with whom we could regularly study Scripture, have fellowship and pray. We wondered whether the Christian love in the Macdonald College Inter-Varsity groups had been a special gift from the Holy Spirit for only that time. Was it a foretaste of heaven probably never to be repeated for us on earth?

But Pastor Ortlund kept stressing the vital need for such a group. The body of Christ had to surround us like a dynamic living organism, he said. There had to be Christians who would take responsibility for us, who would love and care for us, and admonish us when we needed it. There had to be a group to which we would be accountable before God for new spiritual growth in our lives and the group's. In the body each member's spiritual gifts would complete the others. The unity in diversity displayed by the whole group, with Christ as its head, would be a microcosm of the body of Christ in the local situation. Such a group would be the "bride of Christ" described in Ephesians.

That teaching on the body of Christ seemed idealistic, "out of this world"—at least out of our world. There were people in our community we could have asked to join us in a small group Bible study, but our courage was lacking that kind of initiative. Disobediently we left those opportunities slide by us.

During that period of indecision and discontent, Judith arrived in our neighborhood with her husband, Marlin. Judi, vivacious and dramatic, was a nurse by training and an artist by inclination. Her bright personality and inquisitive mind, along with her skill as an international cook, made her dinner parties sparkle. She had spent most of her childhood in conservative, tightly knit Mennonite communities, effectively sheltered from the real world and some of its opportunities and temptations. Now, after graduate school and six years of living in the Caribbean and Asia, she was questioning every theological presupposition she had been taught as a child. Doubt-filled questions tumbled from her: Was Jesus really who he said he was? Was he worth following? Were the Scriptures really written by God or were they merely figments of human imagination? If she was going to follow Jesus seriously, she had to be sure he was who he said he was. "I'm not going to settle for anything less!" she declared.

About six months after her arrival I was at her home for

coffee when Judith said to me, "You and Mark and Tina and Ric seem to be convinced that Jesus is real. Now convince me!" I looked at her amazed. I couldn't think of anything to say. In a torrent of words, she continued, "Why don't all six of you come to my house on Sunday nights and we'll have a Bible study. Then maybe you can do a better job of answering my questions than you can do at Sunday school when there are so many other people to think about."

"Yes, of course," I said lamely. "I'll talk to Mark and see what he says and see if Tina and Ric can find time."

"Good!" she declared enthusiastically. "Sunday night at my house at eight."

I walked back down the hill to our house in a daze. Had she really said that? Was she really serious about finding biblical answers to the questions that always seemed to bubble out of her? What if we couldn't answer her questions satisfactorily? What if she decided she didn't want to be a Christian after all? I felt like a small child with a Woolworth sand shovel, standing before an Everest. Judith knew how to speak her mind forcefully. When Judith spoke, people sat up and took notice. She wasn't cowed by arguments or by political or intellectual credentials. In contrast to me Judith knew how to use heavy earth-moving equipment to deal with people or situations that might seem like mountains to her.

I didn't relish the element of risk involved in starting that small group. At the time I couldn't see it as an opportunity to begin fulfilling my commitment to the body of Christ. Obviously I didn't know much about the Holy Spirit then.

We started that Sunday night at eight, sitting on Judi's patio among hanging pots of exotic, lush ferns and blooming orchids. Candles flickered from interesting holders. Judith, in a handwoven Indian cotton skirt, moved around the patio rearranging a candle, a knickknack or a plant to make it more pleasing to her artistic eye. We were comfortably seated in cushioned, wrought iron chairs and the fans were buzzing overhead, but it was still close and humid on the screened porch. We sat a bit stiffly, fidgeting with our Bibles, making small talk, wondering what would come of it all. Among us, only Judi and her husband, Marlin, seemed comfortable.

I don't remember much of that first meeting except its stiffness. But we did study a passage in Philippians, and Mark and Tina began to answer a few of Judith's questions from it. Marlin, blessed with an implicit childlike faith, wondered why it was necessary to spend several hours hearing answers to questions he wasn't asking. The real wonder of that first evening was that Judith was enthusiastic about meeting again.

We moved the location to our home but continued to meet weekly. Marlin dropped out to babysit his sons on Sunday night, releasing Judith to continue on a regular basis.

Each week we met, sitting on straight-backed chairs around our dining room table, bright lights overhead, the air conditioner and fans humming. Pencils, notepaper and Bibles replaced flowers as the table's centerpiece.

Each Sunday night we would listen for the clip-clop of Judith's Dr. Scholl's sandals on the front step, then the doorbell would ring once and Judith would step in.

"Brrr! Mark must be in charge tonight; it's so cold in here. And I can see we're going to have to work. No sitting on soft chairs tonight!" she teased, as she plopped herself into an easy chair.

Mark's mouth curled into a crooked grin and he shot back, "We'll get more out of it if we work at it. You women are just getting too soft." I ran for a sweater.

Minutes later we would hear the glad rattle of Tina and Ric's Austin coming up the slope and into our driveway. It always gave one last rattle, in protest, after the ignition was turned off. Then their cheery voices would ring out, "Hello! Hello! We're here!" I would let them in and soon we were all seated around the table, Bibles open, pencils poised.

Each week Judith would sidetrack the discussion at hand with question after question. Tina and Mark answered; Ric and I listened and prayed. We didn't resent those interruptions because, after all, that was the purpose of our meeting.

Judith wanted a Damascus road experience. Nothing less.

"It was so easy for those people to believe in those days," she protested. "They saw the signs and miracles with their own eyes. No wonder they were convinced. We have so little to go on. Just the Bible. And what if the Bible isn't true? What if it's just a collection of stories some guys had fun writing?" Her eyes searched each face around the table for answers.

"Don't worry, Judith," Tina assured her. "As you study the Word of God more, you'll become convinced and convicted that God is who he says he is. That he cannot lie. The Holy Spirit will convince you that this is the inspired Word of God and that it's reliable."

After each Bible study we would take some time to pray conversationally about what we had learned that evening. Then we would share some of the joys and struggles in our individual lives, pray for and promise to pray more for one another during the coming week. The next week we would report the progress or disappointments of what had happened that week.

At first we were reticent about sharing our failures, particularly with Judith present. We worried that our honesty would become a barrier, keeping her from taking her own step of faith. After a period of time, however, as trust developed, we couldn't help ourselves. We had to share our lives with one another. When we started telling things as they were, we were also released to pray for things exactly as they were. Things began to happen in our lives as our prayers were answered. And Judith was watching.

About six months after we started to meet we began to notice that Judith was asking fewer doubt-filled questions in the group. At Sunday school she became actually supportive of the authority of the Scriptures when it was questioned. She started to join easily the flow of conversational prayer around the table on Sunday nights. We wondered. Had she really decided to follow Jesus Christ as her Lord and Savior? We knew she hadn't seen any signs and wonders. She would have been the first to report them if she had! No, it seemed that Judith, normally flamboyant, dramatic and vocal, had stepped into the kingdom quietly, even on tiptoe.

I often marveled, and rephrased the words of the old Christmas carol when I thought of her "entering in": "How silently, how silently/ The wondrous gift is giv'n!/ So God imparts to human hearts/ The blessings of his heav'n. No ear may hear his coming,/ But in this world of sin,/ Where meek souls will receive him still./ The dear Christ enters in." He had come. He had gently, quietly given her the gift of himself— and us the gift of a new sister.

It wasn't long after that on a Sunday night that Judith looked around our group and flatly stated, "I think we should invite Enoch to join us. He's so alone, the only Christian student from Nigeria in our church. I bet he'd like to come."

"Yes," we said dubiously. We did have reservations. Ric was a professor in the university where Enoch was a freshman. Enoch was going through severe culture shock and didn't have many positive things to say about Filipinos. How would he relate to Tina and Ric?

Judith brushed our qualms aside, turned to Mark and said, "Why don't you invite him next time you see him?"

So Enoch hesitantly joined us. Because his schooling had been interrupted by the Nigerian civil war, he was our peer in age but not in education. That made him socially uncomfortable at the beginning. But he relished our discussions in the Word; they reminded him of the Fellowship back home in the Christian Union, with students who had prayed and loved him into wanting to follow Jesus Christ as they did. He appreciated having a group of Christians who would now pray him through the maze of exams and assignments he faced each week. The Filipino school system was radically different than the British-influenced one from which he had come.

Later, two couples working with the Peace Corps joined us for short periods of time, and *Ate* Mercy, our church's elderly deaconess, joined permanently. She had been raised in the church all her life, attended a church school and then worked in the church for over thirty years. Faithful. That word would personify her more than any other. A couple of years before, she had been helped into a new quality of relationship with Jesus through a group of Pentecostal Christians. People said she had changed after that. She was no longer just faithful, hard-working and quiet. Now she wanted to talk about her relationship to Jesus. Some said she spoke in tongues. If all those things about her were true, some wondered if she should continue to teach the nursery school administered by the church women's association. Some wondered if she was stable enough. If *Ate* Mercy's heart ached over suspicions cast on her professional competence because of her discovery that the Holy Spirit is a real person, not merely an ecclesiastical garnish in the shape of a white dove, she shared it with no one but Jesus. Her care and love for the little ones increased. Her physical energy to teach two classes full of three-to-five-year-olds was always supplied afresh. In the group we learned to pray for her needs, rejoicing in her loving teaching ministry to children from a half-dozen different countries.

Belenda came next. Her husband Fernando had received a longed-for scholarship to do his Ph.D. in the United States. Belen, however, had not received a companion scholarship, so they had to make the emotionally agonizing decision to split their family geographically for almost three years. Since the political climate on the southern island where they taught was unstable at the time, Fred had insisted that she apply for an inter-Asia scholarship at the University of the Philippines and work on a Ph.D. in entomology while he was in the U.S. Belen had little ambition to start a long, grueling academic trek at that point in her life, especially since she would have to parent their three growing sons alone during that period. She did relish the thought of moving back to our city, largely to have increased opportunity for spiritual growth. She was a new believer, eager to learn more. She laid out a fleece before God. If she got the prestigious scholarship which carried many benefits, including good housing and a generous stipend, she would know it was the Lord's will, as well as her husband's, to begin doctoral work. It seemed an impossible dream. But, miracle of miracles, it came true! Now on Sunday nights Belen joined us.

Often physically weary, she was spiritually vibrant, especially as she told what God was doing in the lives of many graduate students who touched her life. Students felt free to come to her home and talk to her. They could use her spacious apartment for overnight stays and special meetings. She liked the teaching methods and stress on Scripture memorization that Navigator staff workers taught her, and she disciplined herself to study the Word of God regularly using Navigator materials. Being a good teacher, she found it easy to bring illustrations from the materials she was studying into her conversations with students. She seemed to find opportunity after opportunity to present naturally and easily the good news of Jesus' gift of salvation. We learned to pray for many new babies in the faith and we shared the proud joys of their achievements. We also prayed for the parenting problems Belen had with her sons, and helped look after her kids on special outings.

The first Asian Student Missionary Convention was held in the Philippines during that Christmas vacation in 1973. Knowing how much previous Urbana conventions had meant to us, we encouraged Enoch to go along with the delegates from our campus. In the end he was asked to lead a workshop on Africa, so he had to go.

Enoch was given the task of representing the spiritual needs and accomplishments of all of Africa to the Asian Christian students. In preparing his paper Enoch had to learn a lot about Africa he himself hadn't known before. At that time we didn't know what benefits were to come to us because Enoch went to that missionary convention. They were a post-Christmas gift.

Enoch came back all fired up. Michael Griffiths had given a series of morning expositions on the book of Ephesians, concerning the body of Christ and how it should function in the Christian church. For several Sunday nights after that, as Enoch excitedly repreached those expositions for us, we caught his enthusiasm, but the exposition suffered from being secondhand. Finally Judith spoke up: "If Enoch got so much out of Ephesians, why don't we study it now, and see what we can get."

The next Sunday night we started to mine Ephesians. Mark studied ahead of the rest of us, framing good questions that led us to discover the truths in the book for ourselves. What treasures were unearthed as we dug.

When we had finished working our way through Ephesians months later, Enoch mentioned how often the Holy Spirit had been referred to. To most of us, the Holy Spirit was a rather uncomfortable but necessary nonentity. *Ate* Mercy and Belen had had rather dramatic confrontations with the Holy Spirit. But they were sensitive to the rest of the group's feelings at that time so they didn't say much about their experiences. We agreed with Enoch that we didn't really know much about the Holy Spirit, other than his appearance at Pentecost; and that the Scriptures said he gave special gifts to believers, including tongues and healing, which at that time seemed to get the most publicity.

Enoch then volunteered to use his summer vacation to "research the Holy Spirit." After that he would lead a half-dozen Bible studies on the Holy Spirit as portrayed in the Old and New Testaments. Being an engineering student and a somewhat staid Anglican, Enoch wasn't going to get carried away by such emotional controversies as the Corinthian church had been hung up on. Instead, using a concordance and spending many days in the library, he methodically plowed his way through the Scriptures. On Sunday nights we followed the furrow of his learning, looking up reference after reference to the functions of the third person of the Trinity. We discovered how maligned and unknown he had been to us. He represented Jesus to us. He glorified Jesus in all he did in the lives of such followers; he didn't glorify himself. When their lives were cleansed of sin, the Holy Spirit produced the fruit of love, joy, peace, kindness, goodness and patience in their lives, just as a healthy, pest-free, watered mango tree would produce plump golden mangoes. The analogy in the natural world was evident, but we had never realized its applicability to spiritual growth before.

As we worked through the passages on the special abilities the Holy Spirit gives each believer, in order for that believer to fulfill his function in the total body of Christ, we realized that each of us had been given a special ability, a gift from the Holy Spirit. We also realized that some of us had more gifts than others, and that a gift might be removed and replaced with another during certain periods of our lives. Our responsibility was to discover what our gifts were and to use them to build up the body of Christ wherever we were.

Near the end of that series of studies, I came across an article in a *Faith at Work* magazine entitled "Know Your Gift!" It suggested that the small group of believers to which one belonged should help us recognize our gifts if we were unsure of them, affirm our convictions about their presence in our lives and then encourage our use of them. After writing down the total list of special abilities according to Romans 12, 1 Corinthians 12, Ephesians 4 and 1 Peter 4, we each circled on our own list the gifts we thought we had. Later, we discussed them. In our group there was no disagreement about who had which gifts. But someone might be surprised to have others say, "I think you also have the gift of preaching and hospitality. Add those to your list." Another discovery that delighted and amazed us was the wide diversity of gifts in the group. Almost every gift was present, from being able to discern an evil spirit to being able to get people to work together well.

My most releasing discovery through the whole process was to be able finally to accept the fact that I don't have the gift of evangelism. For years I had been whipping myself emotionally because when I tried to act as spiritual midwife in birthing a new Christian, the baby always seemed to be stillborn or the delivery was botched in some other way. I had been guilty of envy toward Belen who, when presiding at such deliveries, did a smooth, professional job of it, bringing a healthy spiritual child into the world, ready to grow. My discovery didn't mean that I was free to live without an evangelistic lifestyle. It meant rather that I should do what I *could* do better, namely, teach and encourage the babies that people like Belen delivered. Belen, on the other hand, was relieved that she could hand young lives over to me for nursing and nurturing. My gift was best used in teaching young people and adults, but Judith and *Ate* Mercy had a special gift of teaching little children. Our son was one whom they taught regularly.

Tina had the gift of giving wise advice as well as helping others. Many people beat a path to her door in their need. Each of us relied on her help constantly. Her gift made ours more effective.

Brother Isaak, a graduate student from India who had joined us, held out his gift of faith to us. He helped us to believe God for things we had never thought God able to do, like giving good computer results for his economics thesis. Somehow I had thought of computers as out of God's range.

"Heresy!" declared Brother Isaak emphatically. "Isn't God sovereign in this universe? Was there anything created that he didn't create? Surely he knows how computers work!"

"Yes. . . ."

"You just pray, that's your responsibility," continued Brother Isaak, "and God will act. You'll see."

God did act. The results were far better than even Brother Isaak had hoped for. And all of us were grateful along with Brother Isaak that Kuya James, a Filipino mathematician in our group, had the gift of helping others. (Kuya means "older brother" in the national language.)

The Scriptures promise that when each member of the body is doing what they are supposed to do, the body will be healthy and growing and full of love. That's exactly what happened. Each Sunday we looked forward to meeting with this small group of brothers and sisters who knew us as we really were. We came with our hurts and heartaches, which were many. But we didn't look only at our problems. We discovered that to have sharing times only, even when we had prayer at the end, left us feeling confused and depressed. We needed to take time to study the Word and see what God said about himself and what he said to us, and how that applied to our situation. After we saw our relationship with God in correct perspective, we could look at ourselves and each other with clearer eyes. The Resource Book was there before us with answers to our problems.

During the second hour, we would discuss our experiences of the previous week, each giving several items to praise God for and several concerns to pray for during the following week. Very often wise advice and help for a particular problem came immediately as other believers around the table gave information or made observations which were part of the solution.

The evening would usually end with long periods of conversational prayer, praising and thanking God for who he is and how he had revealed himself to us through the Bible study that evening. We also prayed about specific items for which prayer had been requested, often praying conversationally around the table for each person present. Then we exchanged lists of individual concerns with another member for special, concentrated prayer during the week. When requests were quite specific, we usually wanted to know as soon as possible the results of our praying for a prayer-partner's needs. Therefore, during the week, if at all possible, we would try to telephone or call on that person to see how Wednesday's difficult employee interview had gone or if the morphology drawings had been completed and submitted by Thursday's deadline. Love came easily and naturally. As we prayed for another, caring for that person was inherent in the process.

As new spiritual babies were born through group members, their spiritual parents brought some of them into our group for teaching and nurturing. Because we lived in a mobile community, people came and went regularly. We understood how the apostle Peter felt, writing his letter "to the saints scattered in. . . ." We knew what it meant to be scattered to the ends of the earth, but always with the glad assurance that some day we would be gathered together again. Today, members of our group during a four-year period have been replanted in Syria, Indonesia, Nigeria, India and elsewhere. The memory lingers of what it meant to have members of the body of Christ care for you and love you. New groups are being formed or searched for.

The experience of putting the people of God, the body of Christ, as the second commitment in our lives was dynamic. We learned what it was like to be completed by working with brothers and sisters within the body. The sense of rugged individualism so ingrained in our American thinking and behavior patterns fell away. We have little appetite left for doing our own thing spiritually. That had become frightening as well as tasteless. There is no attracting beauty by being a single door on a foundation even if the Cornerstone is magnificent. It is still an unfinished building, one not yet fully functional. The temple must be built. "You . . . are joined with him and with each other by the Spirit, and are part of this dwelling place of God" (Eph. 2:22).

10

Culture:
Servant or
Master?

It is far too easy to be an "ugly American." Certain aspects of
our culture, which we practice unwittingly, undo us.

Whether we like it or not, each person, guest and host, is a
slave to his or her own culture to a certain extent. How can
Christians learn to separate the biblically positive aspects of
their own culture from the negative ones? How do we begin to
reinforce what is good and disregard what is unnecessary?

Much has been written about the necessity to integrate and
adapt to the host culture in order to make a meaningful con-
tribution. That was one of the philosophical bases of such organizations as the Peace Corps, International Voluntary Service and Canadian University Students Overseas. Certainly
those organizations have tried to dispel the idea that North
Americans should live like colonial overlords in a country with
a developing economy. Mission societies have taken various

stances on questions of how much their personnel should adapt to local living conditions, the standard of living they will maintain, the amount of language they will learn and the degree to which they will participate in local cultural activities.

For the believer abroad with a business or governmental agency, certain aspects of his living conditions are usually prescribed for him by the agency that employs him. The type of house and the neighborhood may be chosen for him. The make of car he will drive, or in which his family will be driven around by a company driver may come with the job. A person may feel somewhat uncomfortable in the comparative luxury of the provided facilities. But there are two choices: to accept them graciously, be thankful for them and make good use of them for God's glory—or to complain about them and belittle them, as is so often done. Which choice is Christian?

The housing area in which we live is lush and lovely. Pole orchids, birds-of-paradise, poinsettias, hibiscus, and bougainvillea are just a few of the flamboyant tropical plants bordering the well-built American-style houses surrounded by spacious lawns. Most of the residents enjoy gardening, and the Filipino gardeners seem to have a natural eye for artistic gardening.

During the first three years we lived there, I refused to enjoy all that natural beauty. I felt false guilt about living in such verdant loveliness. I feared that if I allowed myself to enjoy it, I might become addicted to it—and then whatever would I do when I had to leave? Ridiculous, yes. Sad, too, because I refused to accept the place, with all its beauty and amenities, as God's gift to me for the period of time he chose to give it.

Living in such surroundings we worried whether Filipino believers would feel free to visit us. Since most of the believers we knew didn't own cars, they had to take public transportation to the guardhouse at the entrance of the housing area and then walk up to our house. That was a rather unsatisfactory arrangement for them because they were subject, in their cultural framework, to *hiya* (shame) for having to walk rather than drive through a wealthy neighborhood.

How could we creatively solve this cultural problem? As we prayed, we saw two solutions. First we prayed that we would be assigned a house as near to the staff housing gate as possible. That prayer was answered. Our home is now the third one up from the front gate. Second, when people phone to say they want to come over, or when we give a specific invitation, we always offer to go get them by car as well as take them home.

The presence of *hiya* in the Filipino personality rubbed us the wrong way for years. *Hiya* is hard to explain, and even harder for a foreigner to understand and accept. It is both a feeling and a value. It is interwoven with the personality and emotional development in a child. In English the word "shame" or the process of feeling shamed only partially describes it. *Hiya* also entails the ego and a necessity for "face saving" actions in a socially or emotionally uncomfortable situation. When people are embarrassed publicly, their *hiya* is affected, often to such an extent that they may nurse a lifelong grudge against the person who hurt them. Such hurts may even demand revenge.

Correcting an employee in the presence of another employee was to provoke *hiya*. The anger of the employer, the gravity of the offense and the degree of embarrassment suffered by the servant determined how much damage was done. Sometimes maids would decide to leave their place of employment immediately after being disciplined by their mistresses simply because they had been embarrassed to such a degree before their peers that they could no longer face them. The mistress was left puzzled and frustrated, because to her the offense might have been relatively small, certainly not something that would deserve such a drastic reaction.

When a maid broke something, even a water glass, she would quietly sweep up the pieces and throw them away. A broken appliance might be hidden. The mistress would not be informed of the accident because the maid was afraid of the possible anger of the mistress and the resultant damage to her own *hiya*.

When I would ask what had happened to a certain vase or why the mixer wasn't working, I would get only an innocent, smiling face as my response. If I pressed further, a soft-spoken "I don't know, Ma'am" would be the only reply. Since they knew the real truth, and I knew that they knew it, I would seethe in helpless anger. Without their cooperation, I could do nothing.

Relief from that frustrating situation came only after girls who were believers worked for me. Then I would painstakingly explain to them that when something was broken, they should come and tell me immediately. I smilingly yet seriously emphasized that I wouldn't be angry if they told me, but I would be angry if they didn't. That argument in itself wasn't entirely convincing to them. What did convince them in the end was an explanation of the network of sin that was spun if they chose to disobey me in that instruction, trying instead to protect their *hiya*.

To hide a broken article, I explained, was deception. During the interval between their hiding it and my beginning to search for it, they had to endure unnecessary anxiety about what would happen if I found the article. When it was found and they felt they had to lie to me further about it, the network of sin became denser. Their lies bred further sin in me: anger and suspicion. The way we could most painlessly extricate ourselves from that whole web of deception was by their honesty and my self-control. As all of us learned those spiritual lessons, the difficulties in our household decreased.

Mark and I were so often outraged with the *hiya* problem in our relationships with many of our employees that for years we insensitively dismissed it. "It's just their egos," we declared. "They'd better learn to be more honest when dealing with us." We used the power available to us as foreign employers to enforce our moral standard with its own cultural trappings, doing what we thought was best. In the process we painfully stabbed many *hiyas*.

To give another example, a written note of correction or reprimand hurts an employee's *hiya* much more than a private face-to-face confrontation. We ignorantly thought that the exact opposite would be a gentler and easier way to deal with discipline problems, especially problems of late, unfinished work or unexplained absenteeism. We avoided face-to-face situations because we were afraid of losing our tempers or saying things that could easily be misconstrued, preferring to write notes where we could choose each word carefully. Not until a Filipino believer told us so did we realize that all our good intentions had the opposite effect.

Filipinos have a sense for being able to determine real emotions, even when we think we are doing a good job of hiding them. That is disconcerting, especially for a believer who is always aware of the Christian witness—or lack of it—carried in interpersonal relationships. One has to learn to repent of one's anger, impatience or judgmental attitudes very quickly when dealing with people. If not, damage is done not only to the relationship but also to the cause of Christ.

Perhaps one reason that Filipinos are so adept at sensing real emotions rather than insincere ones, is that they watch body language. Smiling, face-to-face relationships are highly valued in Asian cultures. Even if your heart is breaking, you still smile. How can you determine the real feelings, the real situation that your sister in Christ is experiencing? Not by looking only at her smile. That is constant. It hardly disappears even when she is disciplining her children. You watch her eyes, the slope of her shoulders or the tightness of her facial muscles. They will tell you more accurately if she is actually relaxed or agitated. It takes time and effort to look for such signs. It is a difficult thing for a foreigner, especially an American, to learn.

Our culture doesn't automatically teach us how to care for others, and how to nurture relationships. We are individualistic, independent and proud of it. We don't look into other people's affairs because we're afraid they will think we are nosey or snoopy.

Mark and I found we had much to learn from the Filipino Christians on how to nurture and care for other believers.

The students often asked one another, "Who are you follow-ing up?" That term meant that you would make a point of visiting the new Christian every day if possible, asking how he was getting along, ascertaining his problems and helping him with whatever he needed—whether a loan of money or some tutoring in math. You had quiet times with him, prayed with him over his exams, helped entertain his relatives when they came to visit or lent him your completed homework if he hadn't finished his before class. (That was to protect his *hiya*. It was a practice that Christians had to be taught was dis-honest.)

It was exciting for us to see how their high cultural value of thoughtfulness in relationships, when harnessed to the biblical command to make disciples, had such power not only to produce growing Christians, but also to draw inquirers into the kingdom.

One Sunday morning Mark and I were both baffled and chagrined to read a note from a graduate student to whom we had previously given some encouragement in her relationship to Jesus.

Her note cited all the opportunities we had had to follow her up in the past two months but had not taken. Now, she wondered, didn't we care about her any longer? She felt hurt and bereft. By our insensitivity to the culture, and to her, we were causing her to stumble. As we carefully reread her note, we could see why she, from her perspective, felt we had been uncaring and selfish. We jumped into the car and drove over to apologize.

One of the things repugnant to Asians about Americans is our "rush-rush" syndrome. Feeling that time is precious we insist on using it efficiently and are scornful of time-wasters. Our habit of rushing doesn't endear us to those who have a different attitude to time.

When believers take a job abroad, they may or may not get much of an orientation course. They may have to become oriented on their own. God, in his providence, was kind to us. He prepared a Filipino sociologist and his wife, both believers to whom the Holy Spirit has given the gift of wisdom, to befriend and teach us. Over the years Tina and Ricardo had had plenty of contact with foreigners, especially American missionaries. They took us under their wings. We didn't realize until our friends told us that our attitudes about time use were repulsive to the Filipinos.

We loved to drop in on Tina and Ric. Their home was always a haven of cheering affirmation for us. We needed their friendship and advice. But we didn't want to take too much of their time. They were both more than fully employed. Relatives, friends and neighbors seemed to stream through their home constantly. We felt guilty about visiting them unexpectedly, yet we needed them often.

The first year we were in the Philippines, we had many frustrating visits like this:

WE: Good evening! Can we come in for just a minute?

THEY: Hello! Hello! Come in! Come in! We're so glad to see you. Children, bring chairs for Auntie Ruth and Uncle Mark. Get some toys for Stephen.

WE: Oh, no, don't bother. We'll just stand here. We're only going to stay for a minute. We don't want to take too much of your time.

THEY: Never mind. Come, sit down. Taste some of this coconut candy Mama has made today.

WE: We can't stay long. We just wanted to ask you. . . .

Ten minutes later

THEY: Please, sit down. We have time.

WE: Oh, no! We can't stay a minute longer. We really must go.

Ten minutes later

THEY: Here, please let us hold the baby. Your arms must ache from standing and holding him all this time.

WE: Oh no, we really must go. It's way past his bedtime.

Ten minutes later

We would reluctantly pull ourselves away, grateful for their time and helpful advice, yet feeling guilty we took so much of it.

Finally one day Tina, seeing that we wouldn't learn by

gentle hints, said to us during one of our standing visits: "Why do you always say that you can stay only a minute? You make us feel that your time is too precious to be spent on visiting with us."

We were shocked. We had been giving a mistaken impression to these dear friends all that time. If they hadn't been believers who knew how to share honestly and forgive, whatever would we have done?

What have I learned about time use?

First, all time is God's gift. Time is not really mine to order as I, and I alone, choose. I must use it carefully, however. I must pray about how to use it. Priorities must be established. Graciousness must be learned when interruptions come, especially in the form of unexpected visitors. As Roy Hession wrote in *The Calvary Road,* that big *I* must be bent into a *C*. I must become willing to go Christ's way rather than my own.

When the sin of always wanting to have one's own way is dealt with constantly, the Holy Spirit cultivates the fruit of peace in a believer's life. That enables me to seem unhurried and unharried even if I had planned to accomplish six errands in an hour but managed only three. It may have been more important to listen to someone's joys or problems along the way than to get everything on my list completed.

Now, if I'm doing an errand that involves entering a home, even if I plan to stay only five minutes, I sit down. I ask about the health of each member of the family before doing my own business with them.

In the local market I force myself to address each vendor I patronize with the proper greetings and farewells. At Christmastime I try to give each one a little gift, such as cookies or a suitable Christian book in their language, to express my appreciation for their service to me.

The problem of knowing when, where and how much to give is a big area of frustration to believers who are "have's" in a "have-not" land. We must learn, first, that all of our resources are God's gift. In our own country how much to give and how much to save doesn't seem to be much of a dilemma.

But in a country with a developing economy, all that changes. We see so much need all the time. Especially at the beginning, we look at everything in the host country through the eyes of North American affluence.

The apostle Paul said that giving is one of the gifts that the Holy Spirit gives to believers. To give in obedience to the Holy Spirit is quite different from giving out of a guilty conscience or to satisfy our own ego. How does one learn to give in a culture in which recipients of gifts from foreigners are suspect and sometimes scorned by their neighbors and relatives? Recipients themselves may mistake the giver's initial motivation. They may feel that the giver is inviting them into a paternalistic relationship. Almost always, the foreigner has no intention whatsoever of becoming a patron to that person. Such a situation would be embarrassing and repugnant.

Excessive or unwise giving can even backfire in an ugly way, the recipient becoming an *oportunista* taking advantage of the giver whenever possible. Being opportunistic does not have a high social value in Filipino culture, but many Filipinos would give grudging admiration to someone who could carry it out successfully with a rich foreigner.

Where does all this leave believers? We tend to be relatively sensitive to the physical needs that we see in the culture around us. We must not, however, allow ourselves to be blinded by obvious material needs. We must learn how to balance spiritual and material need, and minister to both.

One principle we adopted early in our stay was to give only to projects or needs where we personally knew the people involved. So many different educational, religious and fraternal groups came to us asking for donations that hundreds of pesos could easily disappear before we had time to count them. We found that when we politely explained our decision to canvassers for funds, they always respected it. As years went by, we had fewer and fewer canvassers.

Another principle we're learning to follow is that we will not become like miniature gods to people, especially to local believers, by overdoing our giving to them. We don't want them to become dependent on us, rather than on the Lord Jesus, to meet their needs. We want them to learn the excitement of seeing the Holy Spirit provide for them within their cultural framework. Let me share one example of how the Holy Spirit told us definitely not to give to a particular student.

Anesia longed to go to the IVCF-Philippines month-long summer training camp, but the hundred pesos it would take seemed impossible for her to get. She also had to think about her younger sisters at the university whom she was partially supporting. We felt she had definite leadership qualities and we wanted her to go to camp. So we invited her for lunch one Saturday, fully intending to give her the money to go. She arrived bubbling with excitement. Jesus had heard her longing prayers and the prayers of many other students in the IVCF group. She could go to Kawayan Camp after all! One of her professors had offered her a summer job in his lab; she could earn enough for the camp, leave for one month, then continue working for him part-time during the fall semester. Wasn't God kind, she continued, to make her dreams come true for now, and also give her work to help support her sisters on a continuing basis?

Having decided that we would be her benefactors, I found it hard at first to rejoice with her. Fortunately by Anesia's faith, the Holy Spirit showed me my sin quickly. When Mark arrived a few minutes later, he asked me in Low German if I had already given her the money. I replied, "No, God has already answered her prayers. We must say nothing of our intended gift." He was puzzled, but complied. Anesia retold her story to him later.

We rejoiced with Anesia at how the Holy Spirit had answered her prayers and caused her faith in him to grow. Our premature gift in that situation could have stunted her faith rather than helping it develop.

One can find, within any culture, appropriate times to give. Then one should use those culturally acceptable times to the best possible advantage. In Filipino culture there are many such times. If one gives then, the recipient can enjoy the gift without having to endure censure from the immediate community. An example is *pasalubong,* the gift of greeting that a guest will bring to the hostess when he or she is invited or drops in unexpectedly. Usually it is a food item, but it can also be a toy for the children. There were many believers in our community to whom we longed to give. This way we could bring them vegetables from our garden, home-baked cookies or breads (a special treat since most Filipinos don't have ovens), a bunch of flowers or small toys for the children. By using the custom of *pasalubong,* I could easily show our friends that we loved them.

Another custom is that of *pabaon,* the gift that a hostess gives her guests when they leave. Usually it is also a gift of food, often something specially cooked by the hostess. It may be part of the leftovers from the meal that guests and host have shared together. To the many students who visited us, it was easy to give packets of cookies to take back to their dormitories. I was concerned about spiritual input into such students' lives. They often came for biblically directed counsel. Sometimes we would have a book or leaflets on our shelves that spoke further to the issue they had raised with us. Printed matter in the Philippines is very expensive compared with salaries and allowances, so students can't afford to buy much. One day the idea came to me that we should give Christian reading material as *pabaon,* along with the customary cookies. I explained that usually *pabaon* was food for the body, but that we also wanted to give them some food for the soul. They accepted both gladly and gratefully.

Graduations, Christmas, birthdays, baptisms, weddings, anniversaries and funerals are all suitable occasions on which to give. In Filipino culture, during a nine-day period after the burial of a body, friends and neighbors come to the home of the bereaved every evening. The family of the deceased must provide food and coffee for them. That would be a big burden if the custom didn't also demand that the same friends make contributions in cash or in kind to the family. When one of our employees suffered a death in his or her family, we would send money and food items, as well as suitable Christian reading materials in their dialect.

When friends married, rather than giving a household item, we tried to give the couple a mini-library of a half-dozen books, including a recipe book, something humorous, a baby care manual (it is highly desirable in Filipino culture to have a child during the first year of marriage) and some of Walter Trobisch's titles like *Better is Your Love Than Wine, I Married You* and *The Joy of Being a Woman.*

Something that impressed us when we were new in the Philippines was how attractively dressed all the people seemed to be. We discovered that looking as nice as one possibly can is a high cultural value. Coming into the country with our Dutch-German Mennonite background, we tended to be judgmental about that value. Instead, we took pride in wearing our out-of-style clothes. It took us several years to realize that neither our old clothes nor our attitude was especially glorifying to God. We are slowly learning what Eugenia Price wrote in *Woman to Woman,* that we should be neither overdressed nor underdressed in the social strata in which we move. Either way of dressing draws attention to the person, making us rather than the Lord the center of attention.

In the Tagalog area where we live, thrift is not valued as highly as it might be in another area. Again, our own culture, in which thrift is next to godliness, tempted us to be condemnatory toward people who didn't practice frugality. We had to learn not to brag about how cheaply we had bought a certain item, because we only embarrassed our friends rather than having them rejoice with us. It wasn't easy to learn.

For believers in a foreign country, the culture need not be an enslaving and uncomfortable master to which we never know how much obedience to give. Instead, we can master it. Because the Holy Spirit offers us the gift of wisdom, we can expect to enjoy the culture, learn to understand it, and see how to use different aspects of it creatively to bring glory to the God we serve.

11

Cathy: Would She Be Healed?

I first met Cathy on a September Sunday in 1973. She was tall and string-bean skinny. Her blond hair flipped as she skipped along with all the boundless energy of an almost-ten-year-old. Yet there was also a disciplined, studious air about her. I was attracted to her on sight.

Later that morning, at the worship service at the Church Among the Palms, I met her mother, Ruth. She had The Living Bible tucked under one arm. My heart leapt within me. Could it be that another believer had joined the staff of the scientific institute where we worked?

Then Leon, her husband, joined her. He had a scholarly air about him, looking the way I might have expected an agricultural economist to look. He told me he had just been teaching a new college and high-school Sunday-school class. I was amazed. He had hardly been in the country a month and was willing not only to be identified with the local church but also to serve it. That was unusual in our international community.

In the following months, Ruth and I and several other women got together for a Christian book discussion group. We met on Tuesday mornings. As we worked our way through Gladys Hunt's *Ms. Means Myself,* we got to know one another better. As foreigners, each with scientist husbands whose high-pressure jobs left little time for family life, we soon learned we weren't alone. The other members of the group were having problems similar to our own. It was a liberating experience.

During our Tuesday discussions we shared the concerns of our everyday lives. On one of those mornings Ruth mentioned that Cathy wanted to learn to type. Because I had some teaching experience in typing and, even more, because I enjoyed Cathy, I offered to teach her. For three months, as regularly as a well-timed clock, she skipped into my study room at four o'clock, three afternoons each week. She was a delight to teach: well motivated, disciplined and obedient as well as enthusiastic. I looked forward to her coming. We exchanged cookie recipes and talked about the books we were reading.

On Saturdays she often stayed to help me prepare take-home Sunday-school materials for the large nursery class at church. As the class grew from eight to eighteen, she came each Sunday morning to help me teach the action songs, play the new tunes on the little pump organ and help the children with the handwork. Her dependability was a beautiful gift to me each Sunday as I struggled to communicate fragments of the good news to preschoolers from a half-dozen different countries.

By April, when the searing tropical summer had begun, several other preteen girls had joined us to help with the nursery class. Months crept by. One day I looked at all my helpers and thought: "Why don't we have a Sunday-school class just for preteen girls?" By August I was ready to take the leap. I was scared, though, because I had never taught that age group before. Would I be able to communicate God's

Word to them effectively, so that they would want to have a personal relationship with Jesus Christ? Doubts nibbled away at my confidence.

The adult Sunday-school class at our church had had many vibrant discussions that year. Some of the topics under fire had been "The Reliability and Authority of Scripture," "The Deity of Jesus" and "The Evidences of the Resurrection." Cathy's father had asked many searching, provocative questions. My husband Mark, the teacher, spent much effort answering them. We longed and prayed that Leon would take the new step of faith necessary to move from being a good Methodist to being assured of a personal relationship with Jesus Christ.

That August our church sponsored the Lay Witness Mission weekend (chapter 8). When the speaker gave the challenge to stand to signify commitment, whom should I see in the crowd but Cathy and her father, *standing* arm in arm, weeping. It seemed too good to be true.

September that year was wonderful for Cathy and me—except for one thing. The ophthalmologist had discovered that the optic nerve in Cathy's left eye was swelling for no apparent reason. He sent her on to a neurologist, who did further tests. Nothing was conclusive, but something seemed to be wrong, somewhere in the brain. Nobody said much, but we were all concerned and disturbed.

In early October the neurologist ordered that an angiogram, spinal tap and an air encephalogram be done. Judith, a member of our Tuesday Group and the only nurse in our community, flew to her medical textbooks. To her it was obvious: the doctors were looking for a brain tumor. That information chilled us. For one long, agonizing week we twisted that secret knowledge around among three of the couples in our group. Our husbands feared that we were unduly alarmed by the possible complications that could result from each of those tests.

But Judith and I were miserable. What if Leon and Ruth didn't know all the implications? What if the doctors hadn't told them everything? What if something went drastically wrong and we had known that it could happen? We disagreed with our husbands' decision that we shouldn't tell Ruth and Leon what the medical books said. Judith and I prayed, both for peace and for wisdom as to whether we should obey our husbands. If they wouldn't speak to Leon, should we?

The night before Cathy was to enter the hospital for the spinal tap, I finally convinced Mark to make sure Leon knew all the medical implications and possible dangers of a spinal tap if there really was a brain tumor. I was relieved. The next day Leon talked to the doctors and they decided not to do the spinal tap, but the angiogram instead.

That was done two days later. Cathy took it very badly, with vomiting, severe reaction to the dye used and disorientation. The doctors couldn't even finish all the x rays they intended to do. But they did discover that something was abnormal on the left side of her brain because the arteries weren't in a normal pattern.

Then things went from bad to worse. Every day Cathy showed new signs of increasing pressure on her brain. Finally the neurosurgeons drilled three holes in her skull to drain off excess spinal fluid which they felt was the cause of increased pressure. They discovered, however, that there wasn't much extra spinal fluid. Instead, her whole brain was swollen. After that, she was in intensive care, full of tubes, severely disoriented, with a general weakness on one side of her body. She couldn't speak, read or write. She was acting mentally and emotionally like a spoiled two-year-old. The group of believers in our community was stunned. Why had God allowed this to happen to Cathy, her parents and all of us? Why?

That week our Tuesday Group was studying *Prayer Can Change Your Life*. We spent all morning trying to formulate a prayer for Cathy and her family. All the theory we had been studying about prayer suddenly had to be put into serious practice. We were a sober and scared lot.

Sharlene, a member of the Tuesday Group, went around to

all the believers and their children, enlisting them to pray twenty-four hours around the clock. My time slot was three A.M. Each morning for the next three weeks, I awakened without any aid from the alarm. I prayed that God would glorify himself through Cathy's mysterious illness and bring joy to her and all the believers because of what he would do. It was a prayer in sheer obedience to John 16:24, which took all my will power. I wanted to beg and plead with God that he couldn't take Cathy home to himself just now. Whatever would happen to Leon and Ruth's trust in him? What would all our non-Christian neighbors say about all our praying?

The following day Catherine Marshall's *Adventures in Prayer* arrived (by divinely inspired error, I'm sure) from a bookstore in Canada. I hadn't ordered the book, being unaware that it had been published. But they had mailed it anyway. Scanning the chapter headings, I couldn't help but start to read it. It took only to the end of chapter two, "The Prayer of Helplessness," to realize that it was exactly what we needed. We were helpless, all right. I quickly typed up carbon copies of that prayer.

By that time we also had a Friday Night couples' Bible study group. I took the carbon copies to the meeting. Outside, that evening, the tropical night was leaden and foreboding. A typhoon was approaching. Inside, in the cheerfully lit living room sat a half-dozen rice scientists and their wives. Hopelessness seemed to strangle us. Why had this happened to Cathy? Why had medical science failed? Would Cathy get well? If not, how could God allow such a thing?

Mark reminded the group to thank God for the situation as it was, as well as for the evidences of his care in the whole mess so far. Reticence. Then, to the amazement of all of us, Sharlene declared with fiery conviction: "I believe God is going to heal Cathy. I *know* he is!" We looked at her dumbfounded. Hadn't she heard the latest report? Unabashed, she and Mark presented their gifts of faith to us. Gingerly, we reached out to break off fragments for ourselves. Together we prayed "Where are you, Lord?" from Catherine Marshall's book.

Then we walked out into the unwelcome night, mysteriously refreshed.

Our group continued to pray fiercely, but Cathy didn't get better.

By Sunday evening we were desperate. Judith and Sharlene recalled instructions in the book of James to anoint the sick. That concept was alternately embarrassing and frightening for us with our collective Lutheran, Presbyterian, Methodist and Mennonite backgrounds. Finally, it was decided that we must obey the Word of God to the best of our ability. The pastor and elders of our local church were called together. The instructions were clear: "Is anyone sick? He should call for the elders of the church and they should pray over him and pour a little oil upon him, calling on the Lord to heal him. And their prayer, if offered in faith, will heal him, for the Lord will make him well" (Jas. 5:14, 15).

By eight o'clock the group was on the forty-five-mile trip to Manila. The group prayed en route that if this was really God's will, they would be allowed to enter the corridor surrounding the intensive care units and momentarily slip into Cathy's cubicle in order to anoint her and pray for her. On their arrival, the I.C. unit was locked. They rang the call button. The nurse in charge took one look at eight believers who were more fear filled than faith filled. After calling Leon from Cathy's cubicle, they were silently motioned in.

As *Ate* Mercy, Sharlene and Leon stood expectantly around Cathy's bed, our pastor anointed her with oil. Then they corporately prayed the prayer of faith. Leon, who was staying with Cathy in Manila, gave them chocolate cake before their long drive back. A joy-filled lightness spread over the group. They had obeyed God's Word in a new way. The rest was up to him, our loving Father.

Monday, nothing much happened except that Cathy begged everyone from orderly to doctor to be moved back to the room she had been in before the tests. Four-Two-Five. Four-Two-Five. She relentlessly signaled the room number with her fingers. On Tuesday morning her wish was granted.

From that day on she steadily improved. Eleven days later she was allowed to go home, where the doctors continued to treat her medically with steroids for the next two months. How we praised God for the gift of her recovery!

Regular visits to the neurologist and neurosurgeon in succeeding months showed steady progress. The doctors' diagnosis finally was: "General inflammation of the brain from no specific origin." They were puzzled about why she had gotten sick and how she had gotten better, but they were as gratified and relieved as all of us. By January she was ready to go back to school and by May she was promoted to eighth grade.

A few months ago I asked the girls in my Sunday-school class to give their favorite memory verse and tell why. Cathy spoke up immediately, "Jesus' words in Mark 5:36, 'Don't be afraid. Just trust me' are my favorite," she said.

"Why?" I asked.

She looked straight at me and stated quietly, emphatically: "Because I know they're true."

Epilogue

At least once a month I'm on my way back to our city from Manila, alone, with a competent, courteous driver. Sometimes we talk about various aspects of Filipino culture and, often as not, he'll add a few more words to my limited Tagalog vocabulary. But just as often I enjoy a quiet, thought-filled ride. As he smoothly weaves the station wagon through tangled traffic on the narrow concrete road, I pray.

There is thanksgiving for things I have been able to buy and do in Manila. For just the right typing book for one of our maids at a price she can afford. For the happy mother-and-daughter time I had with "Grandma" Irene Shortt over lunch at the Intercontinental. For frozen strawberries to gladden a hungry husband at suppertime.

Sometimes there is repentance. I need to ask for forgiveness for frustration or anxiety because I couldn't get a product or service that had been promised. Or I may have let myself get angry at the Filipinos' cultural value that tries to please by saying, "I'll try," when they really mean "No."

People's needs press into my conscious mind. Things the driver has just told me about his family. The beggar children who knocked on my window. People who have touched my life that day. The doctor who was professional yet caring. A salesclerk, pregnant and tired, who managed a weary smile. The elderly missionary statesman who listened intently, gave wise advice and willingly shouldered my burdens.

There is time for intercession for Stephen and Bethany at home, Mark at the office, each of our maids and each of my neighbors, each fascinating in their uniqueness.

As I look up, my eyes always rest on Mt. Banahaw, "my" mountain, refreshing in its vibrant greenness, season after season. My eyes, trained by now, sweep over the rice paddies nested at the foot of the mountain. Any evidences of insect damage? Oh, I hope not! The mountain rises gently, each crop giving its own shade of greenness to the panorama. The beauty catches at my throat, and I'm glad I don't have to talk.

A part of me lies on this mountain, just around the bend. There in the graveyard stands a tiny, white marble-chip tomb inscribed:

Andrew Klaasen, God's Gift of Love

Nov. 1-3, 1970

Thank you, Jesus.

What a God to have made this mountain and brought me here from the dry, wind-swept Canadian prairies, to teach me about himself. To teach me that in his sovereignty, his creative processes, there is always greenness, new life, new vitality, new hope. I bow my head . . . and worship.